"Melissa and Sissy hav[e] [captured the lan]-guage of the heart of bot[h] [generations. This is a] resource for those who want to understand how to love across the generations, God's way! We have known Melissa over the years as youth leader, mentor, and friend, and Sissy as a gifted counselor and mentor to many teens."

Michael W. and Debbie Smith
Author, Songwriters, and Recording Artist

***

"This book represents years, thousands of hours, of rich, life-changing involvement with teens. It could become a classic."

Larry Crabb
Psychologist, Author and Founder of New Life Ministries

***

"We all want to have good relationships and communication with our teens. In this book Sissy and Melissa share some tried-and-true methods to reach your teen gleaned from their many years of counseling. I think parents reading this will be helped greatly!"

Dennis Rainey
Author and Director of FamilyLife Ministries

***

"If you are looking for practical advice coupled with hands-on experience for raising your teen, look no further. In *The Back Door to Your Teen's Heart*, Melissa and Sissy share how to reach your teen with love and compassion. This is a must-read for every parent!"

David White, M.D.

***

"Sissy and Melissa have helped our television audience for years, and now their secrets of loving and living with teenagers are available for all of us! Having children just entering the turbulent teens, I know what it's like to be 'locked out' of their lives at times. This book is like the 'key under the mat'!"

Debbie Alan
NewsChannel 5 Network, Nashville, Tennessee

"I loved the warm, personal 'backdoor' approach of this book. It is encouraging to parents to know there are dedicated people in this world who are willing to share their expertise in the field of counseling. Thank you both for reminding us that it takes plenty of time, attention, prayers, patience, laughter, and tears to make and keep a family whole! Most of all, thank you for reminding us once again, it takes LOVE—unconditional, Christlike love."

Peggy Benson
Author and Speaker

"This book is amazing! The wisdom, insights and practical advice it contains far exceeds any other parenting book I have ever read."

Cindy Morgan
Recording Artist, Songwriter, and Author

"A must-read for all parents, no matter where you are on your parenting journey. The well-told stories make the wealth of information easy to understand and apply to your own situation. We know that you will enjoy and appreciate this book!"

Brown and Debbie Bannister
Record Producer and Songwriter

"Finally, Melissa Trevathan and Sissy Goff have written down the wisdom and insight gained from their years of work with teens and parents. Since life is too short to learn everything from our own experience, I am so grateful to Melissa and Sissy for passing on their wisdom in such a practical and inspirational way. Their book has the credibility and authenticity that only comes from those who have been doing the heavy lifting that redeeming love requires."

Billy Sprague
Author, Songwriter, and Recording Artist

"*The Back Door to Your Teen's Heart* is an excellent resource! Filled with sage insight and penetrating examples, this book will instill confidence, understanding, and compassion in parents and others who love teenagers. As a parent of teens, I was deeply encouraged and helped by this fine work."

Reverend Michael E. Ellis

"For years, Melissa Trevathan and Sissy Goff have played an enormous role in helping families in our community. Their book speaks to the realities of the lives of teenagers and those who love them. It will engage your imagination and inspire you."

Andi Ashworth
Author of *Real Love for Real Life*

Charlie Peacock-Ashworth, Record Producer and Author of *At the Crossroads*

"This is a book that is so well-written and enjoyable that I read it in one sitting. But the insight on each page is so profoundly helpful that I went back again and again to reabsorb it, a bit at a time."

Sigmund Brouwer
Author

"I would say without hesitation that for me the hardest part of parenting an adolescent is holding on to the slender thread of relationship. Melissa and Sissy offer much wisdom in this area. Their suggestions are worthy companions along the mysterious and often alarming path that leads our children (hopefully) to adulthood."

Ashley Cleveland
Songwriter, Recording Artist

"These two counselors understand both the pulse of a teenager and the heart of a parent. This is a must-read for parents, teachers, and youth workers."

Susan Alexander Yates
Author of *And Then I Had Teenagers: Encouragement for Parents of Teens and Preteens*

"This book takes a thoughtful look at the art of connecting with and understanding an adolescent. Melissa and Sissy have provided a useful tool to reach a teenager's heart in a way that builds a relationship based on respect and unconditional love."

Carter Crenshaw
Pastor, West End Community Church, Nashville, TN

"Piercing the walls and confusion that surround the heart of each adolescent often seems an impossible task. *The Back Door to Your Teen's Heart* offers real wisdom and meaningful insight, but most of all, hope. If your desire is to be the parent God intended you to be, join Him at The Back Door and enter your teen's heart."

John E. VanHooydonk, M.D.
Vanderbilt University

"Wise, rich, biblical and practical, this book will be for parents, grandparents, teachers, and pastors—an essential resource for understanding a teen's heart. It is an excellent tool to help guide us on how to move in and out of their lives through the back door."

Rhonda Smith
Principal, Christ Presbyterian Academy

"As I read this book, I felt as if Melissa and Sissy had given me the rare privilege of eavesdropping on their conversations and relationships with teenagers. Their thoughtful words, loving spirits, and distilled wisdom combine to make this book a compelling and valuable guide into the hearts of youth."

Al Andrews
Counselor, and Coauthor of *The Silence of Adam*

"Through the years of knowing Melissa and Sissy, I have seen their constant commitment to the emotional healing of teens and their families. The way they open their hearts to the children and the parents involved in Daystar paves the way for truly miraculous things to take place. They offer 'real' love and hope in a time when no one's life goes untouched by tragedies—big or small. The passion they share is contagious, their wisdom life changing!"

Kim Hill
Recording Artist

"This book gives tangible, Christ-led ways to engage and relate to adolescents. Through stories, Bible verses, and experience, Melissa and Sissy have written a handbook that every parent and teens should read. It gives parents hope, encouragement, and awareness into the mind and heart of teenagers."

Meg Clark
Director of Camp Waldemar, Hunt, Texas

THE BACK DOOR TO YOUR TEEN'S HEART

MELISSA TREVATHAN AND SISSY GOFF

HARVEST HOUSE™ PUBLISHERS

EUGENE, OREGON

Cover by Left Coast Design, Portland, Oregon

Cover photo: The Image Bank; Ghislain & Marie de Lossy

Author photo by Chuck Shanlever

THE BACK DOOR TO YOUR TEEN'S HEART
Copyright © 2002 by Melissa Trevathan and Sissy Goff
Published by Harvest House Publishers
Eugene, Oregon 97402

Trevathan, Melissa, 1950–
    The backdoor to your teen's heart / Melissa Trevathan, Sissy Goff.
        p. cm.
    ISBN 0-7369-0837-4
    1. Parent and teenager—United States. 2. Parenting—Religious aspects—Christianity I. Goff, Sissy, 1970- II. Title.
    HQ799.15 .T74 2002
        306.874—dc21   2002023272

Printed in the United States of America.

02 03 04 05 06 07 08 09 10 11 / BC-MS / 10 9 8 7 6 5 4 3 2 1

Acknowledgments

This book may have been written by the two of us, but it has been lived, inspired, and supported by a gracious group of folks from across the country. We have been honored to work with the kind staff of Harvest House, particularly Terry Glaspey and Carolyn McCready. Over breakfasts at the Pancake Pantry, with a little prodding over the phone, and through their all-around encouragement, Terry and Carolyn have drawn out something we weren't sure we had in us. We would also like to thank Cindy Morgan and Sigmund Brouwer, dear friends who have stood behind us and pushed from the beginning. A friend who has offered us her vast expertise, calmed us when we've felt overwhelmed, and been an enjoyable answer to prayer has been Jana Muntsinger.

A group of people we feel profoundly indebted to are those at Daystar Counseling Ministry. Our staff and board of directors have propped us up in countless ways over the months it has taken to write this book. David Thomas is a valued friend, skilled photographer's assistant, and the best counselor to boys we know. Kendra Allen has been a strong and steady support... asking us questions and sharing truth from her heart. Pace Humphreys has been our biggest cheerleader, most avid reader, and a treasured friend. Pat McCurdy has patiently held down the fort...all of the while encouraging us and offering lots of chocolate. Finally, we are grateful to a group of kids and families, ages 5 to 85, who have lived out the stories in this book. There are more names than we are able to list, but their faces and stories are indelibly imprinted on our hearts.

Melissa would like to thank Nita Andrews, who shared the vision of Daystar since before its beginning and then helped to make that dream come true. The two men I have learned the most from have been Dan Allender and Larry Crabb. Their teaching is reflected throughout much of this book. To my mother, thank you for teaching me the love of books, laughter, and creativity. To Aunt Robbie, you, along with Mother, have encouraged us with visits, smiles, and turkey and dressing during our writing. To my brother Kim, thank you for sharing your time, wisdom, and experience with us. To my nephew George, you have taught me so much of what I have learned about children and teenagers. To my brother Steve, sisters-in-law, Betsy and Julie, and nephews and nieces John, Sam, Mady, and Libby, I am thankful to be a part of a family that enjoys each other.

Sissy would like to thank her little sister and best buddy, Kathleen. It has been a joy to share with you in the tears and laughter of your teenage years. You are becoming a young woman of tremendous courage, strength, and kindness. To my mom, your love and commitment to me has been part of the foundation of who I am. Thank you for giving me roots and wings, as they say. To my dad, thank you for the sparkle you carry in your eye and for teaching me how to delight in someone. I have felt truly delighted in by you.

Foreword

The topic of adolescents creates a great deal of ambivalence in me. Actually, I am not very fond of them. I have two in the house and one who has graduated from college and is technically no longer in this category. However it is my firm conviction that most of us remain adolescents most of our lives. Perhaps old age—that is, 15 years older than my current age, no matter what age I am—may be the point I transition into full adulthood...but I doubt it.

We are all stuck with adolescents in our heads, hearts, and homes. And to be really honest, it isn't that bad to be around a pack of 11- to 19-year-olds. In fact, one of the most important periods of life is when we simultaneously parent our teens while also remembering the significant memories of our own adolescence. For many of us, eighth grade is a metaphor for hell. For others, the pain, transition, awkwardness, and inherent dorkiness of that period are clouded away and intensely forgotten.

To the degree we forget the unique battles of our past, we will be less likely to navigate well the struggles that our teen is facing. And while their battles appear to be similar, they are profoundly different than our own. Our teens need us to be fully alive and fully human to help them make a transition that launches them adequately prepared into the future.

This is not accomplished by parenting your teenagers as you did when they were younger. It requires more reflection, wisdom, and courage. Things can't be said as directly, and apt teaching moments must arise during the normal course of your relationship, not in a moment of crisis or conflict. This period requires less of us than ever before—less control, less input, less demand, while requiring more openness, hope, and strength.

It is during this challenging time of parenthood that we need wise and gifted guides. Melissa Trevathan and Sissy Goff are women who have spent a lifetime caring for adolescents and their parents. Like brilliant interpreters, they translate the issues of a teen's heart into a language that can be understood by a parent. And in turn, they help parents speak from their hearts to the minds of their children.

I have known Melissa for decades and Sissy for many years, and I know their life passion is to see young men and women grow up in the maturity of Jesus Christ. Their ministry has unquestionably been one of the premier bridge building tools between teens and their families in this country. I trust them and have listened to Melissa as she encouraged me to risk and suffer more for my children.

There is nothing I am or do that matters more to me than being a father and in turn nothing in which I have failed more deeply. *The Back Door to Your Teen's Heart* is a superb book offering me a window into my children's hearts. For that alone, I passionately recommend this book. But, perhaps the most significant gift I received in reading their labor is the sweet, incomprehensible invitation to forgive my children their offenses. And to know the forgiveness of God for my failures. This book teaches great things, but even more it will invite you to the harvest of hope and the wonder of forgiveness that is the most central gift we can offer our children.

You will soon discover the back door is the quickest way to get to the best food in the house. Eat, drink, and enjoy. This is a marvelous book.

> Dan B. Allender
> Author and President, Mars Hill Graduate School

This book is dedicated to our families,
who loved us through our own adolescence

Contents

— ~ —

Introduction   15

Part One: Through the Back Door

1. Maybe You Will Know   29
2. House of Mirrors   47
3. Sound Tracks   67

Part Two: Soften

4. In Here and Out There   85
5. Stargazing   99
6. Love and Laughter   111

Part Three: Shape

7. A Great Big Bundle of Potentiality   131
8. Holding Their Hands, Pointing
   Our Fingers   143
9. A Thankful Heart   161

Part Four: Strengthen

10. Bridge of Hope   179
11. But...   193

Part Five: Going Out the Back Door

12. See You Later   209
13. A Parting Thought   215
    Notes   219

The Back Door
to Your Teen's Heart

Introduction

"How was your day?"	"Fine."
"What did you do in school?"	"Nothing."
"How did you do on your English test?"	"Okay."
"Your dad got a new job today."	"Cool."

To the degree that kids can predict you, they will dismiss you.
Any of us who have ever parented, taught, counseled, or
loved a teenager have felt the fiery sting of dismissal, and
have had a conversation almost identical to this one. In
our offices, we see kids ranging from ages 5 to 18, and our
experience has shown us that adolescence is by far the
most difficult few years in a child's and parent's life. It's
almost as if the child we knew at 10 or 11 years of age—
who laughed with us, went to the movies with us, and
would crawl up into our lap to read a book—has been kid-
napped. The trick on us is that he or she has been replaced
with a child who looks identical, but is often sullen, embarrassed to be seen with us, and seems to speak only in one
word utterances.

Fifteen years ago, Melissa began a counseling ministry
for adolescents. Over the years, hundreds of these teenagers

and their families have walked through the doors of Daystar Counseling Ministries. And over the years, we have learned a lot about what does and does not penetrate the hearts of adolescents and found great success in helping teens and parents learn to communicate. People ask us on a regular basis, "Why don't you start a Daystar in other cities?"

Our response to that question is this book.

We don't believe that every city needs a Daystar. What we believe every city needs are parents, teachers, youth directors, and others who are in relationships with teenagers and are willing to walk through what we refer to as "the back door."

The back door is a concept we discuss regularly with parents who feel dismissed by their adolescent children. It is a metaphor for connection and also the unpredictability of our relationships with our teenagers. It is a metaphor we consider important enough to build a book around.

What we're used to, however, is a front door approach. "You will respond to me because I'm the parent." A parent who comes through the front door states the obvious. With the best of intentions, they take every opportunity possible to teach their children, and always teach with an abundance of words. As a result, they are dismissed by the very children they are trying so hard to teach.

The approach we have found that works best with teenagers is one that comes through the back door. In doing so, we offer both a connection and an unpredictability that takes our teenagers by surprise. A backdoor approach not only surprises our teens, but disarms them in such a way that, before they know it, they have responded without ever intending to.

Connection: The Experience of Relationship

You've probably seen the doormats that say, "Backdoor friends are always welcome." There is a specific reason these particular friends are welcome. They are, indeed, friends. They are people with whom we feel so comfortable, familiar, and connected that they have earned the right to enter our back door.

We've found that the quickest way to be dismissed by an adolescent is to try to be a part of their lives without establishing a real relationship with them. As we try to enter into the life of a teenager, establishing an authentic relationship is crucial. We'll talk about how to do this in the first section of this book.

A mom recently told us of her panic over trying to find the perfect gift for her son, who was going through a difficult time. She had been to almost every store in Nashville. She became so frustrated that she finally just gave up. "I literally fell apart. As silly as it sounds, I just couldn't do it. I couldn't deal with the pressure of finding something that would make him feel better about himself. I felt like a failure as a parent."

Her son's response surprised her. "Mom, you *are* a good parent. I have the best parents in the world."

"That was it," she told us. "From that point, I quit trying so hard. *I started experiencing the relationship rather than trying to make it happen.*"

Through her own failure and frustration, this mom found her way to the back door of her teenage son's heart. She discovered the connection that he was feeling the entire time. But as a parent, part of entering through the back door is to just go on and experience this connection, whether your adolescent responds as endearingly as this boy or not.

Unpredictability: The Surprise of Relationship

Another component of the backdoor image lies in unpredictability. When you come through the front door, you are doing the obvious thing, announcing your presence to all. But this type of approach to an adolescent will often make them withdraw or cause them to become angry and defensive. They may feel more like they've been offered a sales pitch than extended an invitation to relationship. The experience of authentic relationship combined with the unpredictability of the backdoor approach can make a teen feel respected. Several years ago, a teenage girl in one of our group counseling sessions turned to someone who was visiting the group for the first time. "I don't come to Daystar for counseling," she said. "I just come to talk about my problems."

We have heard many kids over the years make similar statements. And when they do, we are thrilled. Our back door at Daystar frequently takes the form of an English sheepdog and a Maltese who are the first to greet each of the kids that walk into our offices. We always have spiced tea brewing in the lobby and baskets full of pictures of our summer camps for people to look at while they are waiting for their session to begin. A majority of kids are not very enthusiastic about their first counseling appointment. But it only takes one lick from our unpredictable sheepdog, Molasses, to soften the hearts of those who've been dragged into our offices. Often these very same kids decide they come to Daystar "just to talk about their problems." Somewhere in the midst of the spiced tea, the dogs, the unpredictability, and the relationships, these kids feel the freedom to open the back door to their hearts and let us in.

Through the Back Door

We hope that this book, in itself, will be a type of back door. It is not about what you can do to "fix" your child. None of us has the ability to directly change the heart of a teen. What we can do, however, is focus on Jesus and His approach to us.

...I have called you friends...
—JOHN 15:15

In this verse, Jesus initiates relationship by making a profound and unexpected statement. He is our Lord and Savior, but He speaks to us in a way that is completely comfortable, familiar, and connected. He calls us His friends.

I stand at the door and knock. If anyone hears
my voice and opens the door, I will come in...
—REVELATION 3:20

We obviously don't know if Jesus is referring to the front or back door. We do know that He is talking about the door to our hearts. And we know that His knock always gives us a choice.

It would be wonderful if we could make every child respond like the boy whose mom was trying to find him the right gift. We cannot and should not try to force a response, just as Jesus does not force a response from us. Even though we may sometimes slam the door in His face, He continues to offer us a relationship with Him. He calls us His friends and continues to knock.

In the first section of this book, we'll describe what it looks like for us as adults to offer authentic relationship to the teenagers we love. In order to offer them relationship, it is important that we first know them. This section will begin by examining the realities of adolescence and the effects of today's culture on our kids. We'll then explore how our response to these adolescents can help them feel respected and lead us through the back door of their hearts.

You're going to be like sheep running through a
wolf pack, so don't call attention to yourselves.
Be as cunning as a snake, inoffensive as a dove.
—MATTHEW 10:16 THE MESSAGE

In Matthew 10, Jesus was literally sending the disciples out to knock on doors. They had a mission. This verse is one that we like to use in our offices for those on the mission we call parenting. Not only does it offer a great description of what it means to enter through the back door, it also provides a little more detail about what we might find at the back door of our teenager's heart.

The Wolf Pack

It may feel like a stretch to think of teenagers as a wolf pack, but if we were to live in their worlds even for a day, we could easily make the connection. As we are painfully aware, violence in schools is at an all-time high; sarcasm seems to be one of adolescents' most common means of communication, and just walking to class, many students are taunted with sexual slurs and belittling comments. Adolescents can be ruthless and cruel to one another and to anyone who tries to get close to them. A middle school girl recently came to one of our counseling groups in tears because of what had happened to her that day at lunch. "I went through the cafeteria line and took my tray to look for a place to sit. I saw the table where my friends were and went to sit down. As soon as I did, every one of them got up and moved to a different table."

The Bible has a great deal to say about children and the importance of teaching and instructing them. With youth, however, the Bible gives more of a mixed message. Scripture refers equally to both the passions and follies of youth. On one hand it describes the strength, vigor, and passion of this age (2 Timothy 2:22, Proverbs 20:29, Ecclesiastes 11:9). On the other, it talks about a recklessness and impulsiveness that can lead to shame later in life (Psalm 25:7, Isaiah 54:4). The intensity present in adolescence may be stronger than in any other period of life. Saint Augustine, one of the most renowned theologians of the early church wrote about the shame and passion of his youth. He said:

> The bubbling impulses of puberty befogged and obscured my heart so that it could not see the difference between love's serenity and lust's darkness. Confusion of the two things boiled within me. It seized hold of my youthful weakness sweeping me through the precipitous rocks of desire to submerge me in a whirlpool of vice!

Strong words. Saint Augustine recognized the intensity of his own adolescence. The intensity teenagers are experiencing can lead them in either a positive or a negative direction, and oftentimes in both at the same time. It is remarkable how many adults point to adolescence as the time when their relationship with Christ began. It is equally remarkable how many adults look back on this period of their lives with shame and regret. This very fact demonstrates the extreme importance of our mission as adults in shaping the lives of adolescents.

The Sheep

In the Scripture, Jesus says we are sheep...not only sheep, but sheep among wolves. Needless to say, this doesn't seem very encouraging. Jesus was, in fact, warning that our mission would be a difficult one. Sheep are known for their helplessness and their vulnerability. Sheep are also known to be harassed by wolves.

A mom we spoke with recently described the first time her 14-year-old daughter rode alone in a car with several boys. The word she used to describe her feeling that night was "terror." She could very much identify with the picture of the kids as the wolf pack, and she definitely could identify with the helplessness of a sheep.

Throughout the Bible, we are described as sheep in need of a shepherd to guide us. And it is because we are so like sheep that Jesus, as our shepherd, tells us how we are to respond.

Jesus sends the sheep into the wolf pack with the charge to be as "cunning as a snake, inoffensive as a dove." The NKJV translates it, "wise as serpents and harmless as doves." The metaphor Jesus uses of the snake and the dove refers to two animals that are about as different as any two animals can be. As the verse states, snakes are cunning and wise. They have the ability to anticipate and outwit their attackers. Throughout the Bible doves are a symbol of peace and gentleness because they are harmless, soft, beautiful, and affectionate.

Wise as a Serpent

If we extend Jesus' image to parenting, it would imply an awareness of the culture in which teenagers are living. If we understand the wolf pack, we can be wise and unpredictable in our response. For example, a teenager comes home from church and announces that she is no longer going to be a part of her youth group. "Everyone there looks alike, dresses alike, and won't talk to anyone new. Besides, I'm not even sure I believe in that stuff anymore." Such a statement could be a difficult blow for the parent of a teenager. Most adolescents expect their parents to respond by coming in the front door and giving them announcements, not choices.

- A **front-door response** would be something like, "Youth group is not negotiable. You will be a part of your youth group as long as you are living under my roof."

- A **backdoor response** that is unpredictable and wise could be one such as, "That's fine. You don't have to go to youth group anymore. You can choose between youth group, Young Life, FCA, or a small group Bible study. Whichever one you choose will be fine with us."

The unpredictability of the back door is in the offer of a choice. The snakelike wisdom can be found in the fact that, in the midst of making her own choice, the child will still be attending some kind of Christian activity. The parent has allowed the child to make her own choice but within the context of his or her own priorities as a parent.

Harmless as a Dove

The dove, in contrast to the snake, offers the gentleness that is found in connection. A teenage boy who had been suspended from school told us in group about a conversation he had with his father when he came home. In a soft voice, he said, "When we were talking, my dad put his hand on my shoulder. I remember thinking, 'I don't ever want him to take his hand away.'" This dad had a strong conversation with his son about what he had done, but it was carried out in a context of relationship and connection that moved the heart of his adolescent son.

To be both a snake and a dove is a way of walking through the back door of a teenager's heart. In the verse in Matthew, Jesus says, "You are going to be like sheep running through a wolf pack, *so don't call attention to yourselves.*" To only be a snake and to announce our power as an adult is like pounding on the front door, trying to barge our way in. We call attention to ourselves. To only be a dove would never earn the respect that allows us to be heard. We would be dismissed.

In many families one parent acts as the snake and one parent acts as the dove. But this is not the goal we're working toward. A child who has one snake parent and one dove parent will end up playing the two against each other. They will eventually come to dislike the snake and dismiss the dove.

As parents, teachers, counselors, and adults who care about adolescents, it is our mission to be both. The combination of unpredictability and relationship we offer are what free the adolescent to respond. As teenagers begin to respond, we can help them move through three stages on the road to growth and maturity—softening, shaping, and strengthening.

Soften

Softening is the first thing that takes place once the back door is open. Part Two of our book will describe what softening looks like in the life of a teenager. Softening means creating a place where teenagers can feel safe and free to be honest about their world and about themselves. It involves reminding them that they are not alone, that we enjoy and care about them deeply.

Shape

Part Three of our book will talk about shaping. Shaping seems to be the part that we often feel most comfortable with as adults. Shaping means helping them to learn, to grow. In the context of a safe relationship, it means helping to mold them into who God has created them to be. This doesn't happen by coddling them or by forcing them to learn, but by respecting them in a way that says, "You are created for much more than you are now experiencing."

Strengthen

The fourth part of this book will look at what it means to strengthen all that God has been doing in the lives of our children. Strengthening means helping them see that they have a voice. It means reminding them that nothing is ever so terrible in their lives that they don't have something to give to others. Every teen longs to know they make a difference, and we can be instrumental in giving them opportunities to do so.

Strengthening cannot come before shaping, and shaping cannot take place without softening. And none of these are possible if we are not invited into the back door of the adolescent's heart. It is our hope that this book will help you to reconnect to the teenager that you know and love and to discover new things about yourself in the process. It is not, however, a three-step process we work through once and for all. We will join our adolescent friends in continually being softened, shaped, and strengthened by God until we meet Him face-to-face and are all made perfect.

Going Out the Back Door

The final section of our book will address the importance of giving our teenagers room to grow. As we walk out the back door of their hearts, we help them to establish independence, as well as a dependence on God. The quality of relationship we have established with our children gives us the freedom to leave and to return, and gives them a foundation on which to grow.

Picture a teenager sitting in his den, feet up on the coffee table, watching television. Someone knocks on the front door. He gets up, walks to the door, and looks through the peephole before he even considers opening the door. If he doesn't know the person, he possibly goes right back to his spot in front of the television.

Now, imagine someone knocking on the back door. This time, he simply looks toward the door and says, "Come on in." He hollers again, in a louder voice, "Come on in. The door is open." The person on the outside steps in...

Part One

Through the
Back Door

1

Maybe You Will Know

———

Three things amaze me, no, four things I'll never understand—how an eagle flies so high in the sky, how a snake glides over a rock, how a ship navigates the ocean, why adolescents act the way they do.

—Proverbs 30:18-19, The Message

It wasn't just Solomon who was amazed by adolescents. Every parent, teacher, counselor, and adult in relationship with those aged 12 to18 feels completely baffled at one time or another. It is for this reason that we loved Peterson's unique translation of this verse in Proverbs. None of us understands why adolescents act the way they do. Getting through the back door of teenagers' hearts doesn't seem to be much of an issue for us. We feel like we can't even find the right house.

And understandably so. The bodies of adolescents are changing as rapidly as their tastes in music, and raging hormones are dictating a great deal of their emotional state. They are only beginning to be able to think in terms of the abstract, but they are, nonetheless, strongly opinionated, even if those opinions seem to change overnight. One minute, they may resemble a 25-year-old, and the next, have a remarkable similarity to a two-year-old. Researchers have recently discovered that the brains of teenagers are still developing. As *U.S. News and World Report* stated, "The adolescent brain is far from mature. Just as a teenager is all legs one day and all nose and ears the next, different regions of his brain are developing on different timetables. For instance, one of the last parts to mature is in charge of making sound judgments and calming unruly emotions."

Of course, this doesn't come as a surprise to anyone who has ever loved an adolescent. Adolescence is a period of profound change—physically, emotionally, mentally, and spiritually. And because of all the change teenagers are experiencing, we often feel at a loss as to how to connect with them. To enter through the back door sounds like a wonderful idea, but we seem to have lost our teenager's address. *In order to find the right house and walk through the back door, we need an understanding of adolescence itself.*

For most of us, a few years have passed since we experienced life from an adolescent's perspective. Even if we can remember what it felt like to be laughed at during gym or to have our first date, the culture teens live in has changed to such a degree that it is difficult for us to relate. Therefore, it may be helpful for us to become their students. In this chapter, we'll take an in-depth look at who teenagers are, what they want, and how they usually go about getting it.

Melissa has a nephew who, at age seven, was both highly intelligent and highly impatient. One afternoon he and his grandmother were running errands. After quite some time, George decided he was ready to go home. His grandmother responded that she just had to make one more stop at the grocery store. He proceeded to throw quite a fit. His grandmother quietly took a piece of paper and a pen from her purse and said, "Here, George. Why don't you just write a poem?" When George's grandmother returned from the store, George took the piece of paper, threw it at her, and said, "HERE!"

> My urge is yet to feel your grip and see you once
> again, And yet I don't know why my urge is so.
> Maybe you will know.

These are uncharacteristically powerful words from a seven-year-old. George may not have reached adolescence, but the words he wrote reflect not only the longing and confusion of teenagers, but also our calling as adults in their lives. Teenagers do not understand all the changes and feelings tumbling around inside them. But they want us to. They want us to have enough knowledge of who they are, what they want, and how they go about getting it that we will do our best to understand. Then, as Solomon says in Proverbs, we can stand back and "be amazed."

Who They Are

Changing

It can be a difficult task to determine who teenagers are, because who they are can change without a moment's notice. Sissy had been counseling a 16-year-old girl for several months. Her parents were very concerned about her attraction to the "gothic" look. (Kids who dress gothic tend to wear all black, very baggy jeans, lots of dark eye make-up, and chains and spikes as accessories.) This young woman's attitudes had begun to mirror her style of dress. She kept her head down, her hair covering most of her face, and scowled when anyone tried to speak to her. Then one day she practically skipped into Sissy's office. She was wearing a bright yellow T-shirt with a smiley face, lots of multicolored bracelets, and significantly less eye makeup (although she still had on the baggy jeans). When asked about the tremendous change, she simply said, "I got tired of being gothic. It was too depressing. I decided to be a skater instead."

Development has been defined as bringing out all that is potentially contained within us. For adolescents, this development can bring out things that, as adults, we do not necessarily want to see. We have heard many parents of teenagers say, "I hate to say this, but I don't even like my child right now. He barely speaks to me, and when he does, it seems like all we talk about are consequences and curfews." Teenagers are working frantically and, sometimes furiously, to define their own identities. In so doing, they will sometimes delight and many times offend us. But this search for identity is a crucial part of the process of growing up.

Ambivalent

Adolescents are living in a constant state of ambivalence. They long for intimacy but are afraid of it. They are trying to develop their own identity but still want to cling to their parents. They want freedom but within the confines of safety. They are continually saying, "Come close, get away." In many ways, teenagers are not that much different from toddlers. They want their independence but are always checking to make sure we are watching.

Because of this attitude of ambivalence, of not really knowing what kids want, the period of adolescence can be as confusing for the adults as it is for the adolescents. In the morning before they go to school, teenagers may be saying, "Come close." They want to eat breakfast with us. They want us to talk with them about their day on the way to school. Then, if we don't tell them we love them before they get out of the car, their feelings are hurt.

"Get away" may be the only thing we hear from our children when they get back in the car after school. They won't answer any of our questions. They barely look at us, let alone smile. Having adolescents can spin many parents into a period of either feeling highly insecure or laying down stricter boundaries for their children. If we feel that their mood swings have something to do with us, we may plunge into depression thinking that they no longer like us. We may blame all the changes on their friends. In our offices, we hear many parents say, "He never acted like this until he started hanging out with this new group of friends." If we feel this way, we may get into a panic and want our child to do something drastic like change schools midyear. Or, we may just feel like our own child has gone haywire. Overnight they seem to have turned into a difficult, disrespectful child. If this is the case, we will most likely spend a lot of time punishing or simply being angry with them for their attitude.

We cannot emphasize enough, however, that ambivalence is a normal part of adolescence. Almost every teenager will go through a phase of saying, "Come close, get away." But it can help us cope if we remember that even in the "get away" times, they are still looking back to see if we're watching.

Self-absorbed

This is another integral part of a teenager's development that can be quite frustrating for the adults in their life. For many of us, if we were to choose one word to describe the adolescents we know, it would probably be self-absorbed. Again, this is also a very natural part of their development. One family we work with has a son away in college and a 14-year-old daughter. Several months ago, the children's grandmother, whom they were very close to, died unexpectedly. The mother of the two children recounted for us a conversation that took place between the son in college and his younger sister.

"Hey, Mary, I just heard about Grandmother. I wanted to call and see how you're doing."

"I'm fine. How are you?"

"Well, (long pause) I'm pretty sad, like I'm sure you will be at some point. I also wanted to tell you that I'm trying to catch a plane home tomorrow to be with you and mom and dad."

"Oh, I'm so excited. That means you'll get to meet Josh, my new boyfriend."

The last thing this young man was thinking about at the time of his grandmother's death was his sister's new boyfriend. It was, however, the first thing on his teenage sister's mind. Adolescents spend most of their time dwelling on their own lives—their changing identities, their changing looks, and how other people perceive them.

Theorists have come up with a term called an "imaginary audience" that is specific for this age group. Teenagers walk through life thinking that a throng of people are watching their every move and waiting for them to look foolish. They believe this "imaginary audience," for example, would laugh if they saw them going to the movie with their parents or walking through the mall with their brothers and sisters. This struggle to find their own identity as separate from their parents coincides with their heightened concern over what others think. As a result, peers' voices become the ones that adolescents listen to with the most intensity. After all, they spend the greatest portion of their time either in the company of friends, talking with friends on the telephone, or more recently, instant messaging each other over the Internet. All this time invested in relationships is a large part of a teenager's journey to discover his identity.

Impulsive

A vivid illustration of another teenage characteristic is one that Jesus describes in Luke 15. He tells a story familiar to many of us about a man with two sons.

> *The younger one said to his father, "Father, give me my share of the estate." So he divided his property between them. Not long after that, the younger son got together all he had, set off for a distant country and there squandered his wealth in wild living.*
>
> —LUKE 15:12-13

The Prodigal Son may not have actually been an adolescent, but he was definitely impulsive. In his desire to be independent, he asked for his inheritance and left the safety and security of home. After he arrived in a distant land, he "squandered his wealth in wild living." The Prodigal Son was impulsive in his decisions...impulsive enough to quickly spend his way through his own inheritance. If we were to hand over our bank accounts and credit cards to our own teenagers, it would probably not take them long to do a little squandering themselves.

We have all seen this impulsiveness in our children—and not just in the area of finances. It might also be in the area of automobiles. A teenager may say, "I need the car and I need it right now. It doesn't matter if I don't have a driver's license." We will find this child sneaking back into our house early in the morning or being brought in by the police. Another teenager may say, "I didn't have time to study for this test. I'll just look on to Susan's paper. She always gets good grades." This child will either get caught and receive a zero or risk being expelled. The impulsiveness of teenagers comes from a feeling of desperateness that says, "I want, I need, and I'll do whatever it takes to get it...RIGHT NOW!"

Impulsiveness, self-absorption, changing identities, and ambivalence seem to be themes common to all adolescents. Almost every teenager we have met struggles profoundly with each of these issues. We do not believe, however, this sums up all of who adolescents are. As we outlined in the description of the wolf pack in the introduction, teenagers are also intensely passionate. The combination of these factors makes adolescence one of the most difficult times any of us will ever experience. Not only are teenagers' lives often in a state of upheaval, but they do not have the emotional maturity to handle what they are going through. As adults, it is our challenge to see through the confusion of who they are to what they actually want.

What They Want

Several years ago, Melissa met with a mother who had just given birth to her second child. Her son, who was around the age of seven, was having a difficult time adjusting to the idea of no longer being the baby of the family and the center of attention. His mother arrived home from the hospital to a crowd of relatives who had come to admire the new baby.

Everyone in the room was caught up in the excitement of the baby when the young boy walked into the room and said, in a determined voice "Hey, if there's anybody here who loves me, raise your hand."

This young boy wanted attention. He wanted to know that he was still loved as much as he had been before his mom came home with a new baby. And he had the courage to say what he wanted. Teenagers, on the other hand, tend to make us guess. They want, just as strongly as this boy did, to know that they are loved. But instead of expressing what they want, they may act indifferent or even express the opposite. We will discuss more about the way adolescents mask their feelings later in the chapter. But first, we would like to take a more in-depth look at what adolescents really want.

Safety

All of us want to know that we are loved and accepted for who we are. We would all, at one time or another, like to just stop and say, "If anyone here loves me, raise your hand." For many teenagers, though, being accepted for who they are seems like an entirely foreign concept. As we have said before, their moods are as varied as their opinions. They are sometimes angry, sometimes impulsive, sometimes detached, and sometimes delightful. They are often feeling both real and imagined rejection from peers and experiencing an increased level of academic pressure to perform. Social pressures are pushing them to either be a perfect example of a well-adjusted adolescent or a rebellious teenager who rejects adult culture. As a result, these teenagers can sometimes plunge to depths of extreme self-hatred. And when they're feeling such strong self-hatred, they will many times act out.

Larry Crabb, a Christian psychologist and mentor to Melissa, said that kids are asking two questions—"Am I loved?" and "Can I get my own way?"—and they are asking them both at the same time. *The parents' responsibility is to assure them that "YES, you are loved and NO, you cannot get your own way."* Safety, for the adolescent, is a combination of security and boundaries, not just one or the other.

As adults in the lives of these teenagers, it is of vital importance that we respond to these questions. Teenagers are not likely to ask them directly. They will ask them by forgetting to clean their room or by staying out 30 minutes past their curfew. Whatever the situation, it is important for us to answer the questions. And in the midst of answering, it helps if we have our hands raised.

Relationships

Adolescents are not only becoming aware of their need for safety. At this age their eyes are opened to many of the realities of life, realities that can be both exhilarating and profoundly disappointing. In her book *A Circle of Quiet*, Madeleine L'Engle describes an experience of her eyes being opened to an awareness of the reality of others.

> And that was my moment of awareness: that woman across the court who did not know me, and whom I did not know, was a person. She had thoughts of her own. She was. Our lives would never touch. I would never know her name. And yet it was she who revealed to me my first glimpse of personhood. When I woke up in the morning the wonder of that revelation was still with me. That afternoon when I went to the park I looked at everybody I passed on the street, full of the wonder of their realness.[1]

Watching her neighbor through her bedroom window, Madeleine L'Engle realized that life existed outside of herself. At some point during their adolescence, so will each teenager. As their eyes are opened to the reality of others, they will also be opened to a need for deeper connection.

For teenagers, becoming aware of their longing for relationship can feel like being ripped in two. Because they have an almost exaggerated need for independence from their parents, they also have an exaggerated need for attachment to a peer group. The problem is that the relationships they see as most important are the ones that are the most tumultuous. All adolescents are going through similar turmoil, and therefore will often take their pain and confusion out on each other.

"For the first two weeks of school, she told me I was her best friend," one teen might comment. "Now, she won't even look at me in the halls." Friends betray other friends without any notice or reason. Girls often complain about getting dropped by other girls who begin serious dating relationships with boys. Boys are dropped because they don't make the football or basketball team at school. As friends are becoming all-important, they are also becoming inconsistent, and rejection feels like the ultimate blow.

The relationships that adolescents are moving toward include those with same-sex friends, members of the opposite sex, and those that signify belonging to a group. Having a "best friend" is a very significant issue for teenagers. We have heard it said many times, "It's not that I don't have friends. I just don't have one that I feel really close to." Teenagers' need for connection, combined with their raging hormones, can lead to very increased interest in the idea of a boyfriend or girlfriend. Many teenagers will begin to spend considerable amounts of time with members of the opposite sex. Many will wonder, "What's wrong with me?" if they don't.

Within a group of friends, adolescents often find their sense of belonging. Their need for group acceptance is not only why cliques exist in schools, but also why these same cliques are destructive to many teenagers.

In the midst of the relational turmoil, every adolescent needs to feel that they have a haven. They need to know that at least one relationship exists in which they can feel safe. As adults we can provide this, pointing them toward One who will never leave them or forsake them.

Faith

- "It just seems like I don't have anyone who really cares."

- "I feel like there are people who care about me, but they just don't care enough."

- "No one understands how alone I feel, even with all my friends around."

In one of our recent high school girls' groups, several of the girls talked about their loneliness. Their eyes were being opened. They were not only disappointed in their relationships, but were becoming aware of a hunger that no one person can ever fill.

During our summer camps, most of those who make commitments to Christ are teens. Because they are experiencing a disappointment that simply will not go away, teenagers begin to search in ways they never have before. They see that life is not as clear-cut as they had once believed and that things are not necessarily as they seem; they are much more complicated. It is a critical period in which they are able to integrate the realities they are now seeing with their own sense of faith.

"I grew up with Christianity being absolute truth in my family. It was all around me. I never thought about questioning it before. Since my boyfriend and I broke up, I've been doing that. I've been struggling, and it's been so good. It's been hard, but it's been really good. I feel like I really am finding my own relationship with Christ, not my parents'." The eyes of this senior in high school had been opened by the breakup with her boyfriend. She had hurt deeply. As a result, she began to search and discover Christ with a fervor she had not known before.

Meaning

As well as needing safety, close relationships, and their own sense of faith, teenagers also have a strong need to know they make a difference. A high school student came in to meet with Melissa, sat down, and immediately said, "Will you rake me?"

Melissa looked at him with a puzzled expression and asked, "Rake you?"

"You know, like you rake Brent, Kerry, and Jim over the coals."

What this young man was asking was for Melissa to challenge him, just like she had done with the boys he mentioned. He knew that if someone called his hand on what he was doing, it would mean that they believed in him and who he could be.

Each adolescent longs to feel that his or her life has meaning. They want to know that someone believes in them and feels they are capable of greatness. Watch any teenage boy in his back yard practicing basketball. "He comes in for the lay up. He shoots and IT'S GOOD! And the crowd goes wild! YEAAAAA!" This boy is seeing his life as meaningful, at least in the eyes of the imaginary crowd watching him shoot.

As children move into adolescence, they begin to ask, "Does it really matter that I'm alive? Can I or do I make a difference to anyone?" For younger adolescents, these questions can be answered by success in basketball, good grades, making the school play, rock climbing, playing the drums, or being a part of a team. Being involved in different kinds of activities can create a sense of confidence in early adolescence.

In later adolescence, these questions take on a deeper meaning. Older adolescents start to see that the activities don't fulfill them anymore. They yearn for something greater. Girls decide they want to quit taking piano lessons. Boys don't spend as much time throwing the football. Their eyes begin to be opened to the possibility of something more. At this point, they can either become bored or allow themselves to be drawn to something deeper. Older adolescents find purpose when they see that their lives can be meaningful to someone else. They may spend hours on the phone helping a friend get through a hard time. This helps them feel a sense of purpose. It's about one life touching another. It is discovering that God can really use them. It is the process of strengthening we mentioned in the introduction.

How They Go About Getting It

In June 1986, a collegiate track star was competing in the NCAA Track and Field Championship in Indiana. A pre-med major and a member of the Dean's list at North Carolina State, this young woman had great plans to be a medical missionary. Just six weeks earlier, she had broken the collegiate record for the 10,000-meter run. When asked about her accomplishment, she replied, "One thing that has helped me is not placing so much importance on my performance in trying to please other people. I just have to learn to do my best for myself and for God and to turn everything over to Him." On the day of the championship race, she was running with a group of women in the lead of the race when suddenly and without warning, she ran off the track. She proceeded to jog across the softball field and run straight to the New York Street Bridge, which she immediately jumped off. Thankfully, she survived this tragic event.

We do not know this woman, have not spoken with her, and do not know what actually prompted her to jump. We can, however, make some guesses based on what we know of adolescence. This young woman's words surrounding her record-breaking race sound so right. Reading them, we feel both encouraged and inspired. We also hear the voices of scores of teenagers who are afraid to verbalize what they want. Most adolescents, just like the rest of us, would like not to worry about their performance or about pleasing people. We would like to turn everything over to God and never think about it again. But we haven't come across anyone who could actually do this. Of course this young woman wanted people to respond to her. Of course she wanted to perform well in the thing for which she had spent countless hours and days training. And with the pressure she was putting on herself not to feel these things, she could easily have been at a point of hopelessness.

> *As the deer pants for streams of water, so my*
> *soul pants for you, O God. My soul thirsts for*
> *God, for the living God.*
> —PSALM 42:1-2

The truth is, we are a hungry and thirsty people. We do want. Throughout the Bible, and especially in the Psalms, we see references to a hunger for relationship with God, a thirst for joy, intimacy, and even darker emotions such as revenge. The hunger experienced by teenagers is even more intense, because their eyes are just becoming opened to the reality that their hungers and thirsts are not being fulfilled. Therefore, adolescence is a time when many turn to a personal relationship with Christ. Because the hunger of teenagers has taken on an even greater intensity, so has their search. They are more likely to develop deep friendships. They are more likely to look to these friends and to members of the opposite sex to fill their hunger. And when the hunger gets to a level that is uncomfortable, they are more likely to do whatever they can to avoid the hunger at all costs.

So how do adolescents go about getting what they want?

Deny

Like the young woman in this story, many adolescents will try to deny their longings. They may do so through some of the more rebellious and obvious ways such as drugs, alcohol, sex, or pornography. In our counseling offices, we have noticed an increase in the number of kids who are experimenting with eating disorders, self-mutilation, and homosexuality as ways to deny their longings. Some of the more performance-driven teenagers, however, will choose ways that are unnoticeable to outsiders. They will simply take their hearts and disappear inside themselves. These adolescents may make wonderful grades, be leaders in the student body, and even be enjoyable to their parents, but at some level there is a vacancy inside.

Almost all teenagers that come into our offices are brought by their parents. An adolescent will not often say on their own, "I have a problem and need to talk to someone." More often than not, it is the parent who seeks help. Many of those who are brought in are experimenting with the things that we just mentioned. Some are detached. And others are doing their best to become either tough or cool so that no one will know what they are feeling. The words we hear most often from those whose parents are either separated or divorced are, "I'm used to it." But more and more statistics point out that they are *not* used to it and are being profoundly hurt by the pain they are trying so desperately to ignore.

Demand

Another way many adolescents respond to the intense hunger they are experiencing is to demand that someone else fix it. Melissa was meeting with an adolescent girl and her mother several years ago to discuss problems in their relationship when the daughter raised her voice and said, "I just want to be loved CORRECTLY." So do we all. Teenagers, however, are not yet able to see that no one will ever love them enough to take away their loneliness or their pain. As a result, they either demand or make attempts to manipulate us and the situation so that they will feel loved.

A boy involved with Daystar once told us that when he was feeling lonely on retreats he always did the same thing. Afraid to acknowledge his hunger and afraid to tell someone he was hurting, he would instead walk out onto the dock over the lake and wait for someone to come and ask him if he was okay. We have used this as a metaphor countless times with adolescents. They are continuously walking out onto docks, hoping that someone will come out to love them, and love them correctly.

As we all know, each attempt adolescents make to deny their hunger eventually fails. The alcohol and drugs wear off and the loneliness remains. The girlfriend decides she is in love with someone else, and the adolescent boy feels that something inside of him is missing. Someone follows us onto the dock the first few times but eventually grows tired of the chase. None of it works for long.

When teenagers begin to recognize their attempts as failures, the pain that follows is very real and very intense. They may feel a helplessness that says, "I am afraid I'll never stop being sad." They may feel worthless and think, "What is wrong with me?" They may experience a loneliness that says, "There is no one else in the world that feels like I do." And how they respond to these feelings will often determine how they choose to live.

Move Toward Christ

In the Psalms, David talks about his thirsts. He doesn't deny them or demand that someone else come to his rescue. Instead, he calls out to God. One of the same girls who talked in group about her loneliness has just begun this process.

"I still don't feel like anyone really cares," she says. "I still feel really alone. But, I've started reading a book called the *Ragamuffin Gospel*. In my loneliness, I really want to learn how to look toward Christ." What she said is very simple. She is acknowledging her hunger and thirst. She is letting go of her demand for relief. And she is taking her hunger and thirst and moving toward Christ.

How We Can Help

The minister is not called to cheer people up but modestly to remind them that in the midst of the pains and tribulations the first sign of the new life can be found and a joy can be experienced which is hidden in the midst of sadness.[2]

—HENRI NOUWEN, *THE LIVING REMINDER*

As parents, teachers, counselors, and those who love adolescents, we can be their reminders. Through our lives we can show them the first signs of new life. In the midst of their hunger, their thirsts, and their sadness, we can remind them of the joy that can be experienced this side of heaven.

Adolescence is a time of profound change and profound disappointment. Teenagers are learning their own limitations and the limitations of those around them. It is a natural time of letting go of the ideals of perfection and recognizing the need for more than this life can offer. It is a very painful time for them and for us as we watch them struggle. As adults who care deeply about these adolescents, we have a challenging and exciting task before us. Adolescence is our time to encourage the questions, the struggles, and the longings and to help guide these kids to something far greater than the childhood they are leaving behind. As we come to know the adolescents we love and to understand what they want and how they go about getting what they want, we begin the process of walking through the back door of their hearts.

2

House of Mirrors

———～———

In mirrors I see myself. But in mirrors made of glass
and silver I never see the whole of myself. I see the
me I want to see, and I ignore the rest....Mirrors that
hide nothing hurt me. But this is the hurt of purging
and renewal—and these are mirrors of dangerous
grace.[1]

—WALTER WANGERIN, *RELIVING THE PASSION*

Several years ago, Sissy met with a mother and daughter
who were going through a time of conflict. Their meeting
started off rather calmly, with each saying what she felt the
problem to be in their relationship. It progressed quickly
to a shouting match, with each saying what she felt the
other's problem was. "Mom, you're so mad all of the time.
I don't even know why," the daughter said. In the midst of
the argument, the mom started sobbing.

"I finally see it," she said. "I don't know why I haven't
realized it before. All of the things I get mad at you about
are things I don't like in myself. Somehow, you just bring
them to the surface."

This is not to say the problems were entirely the mom's
fault. The teenage daughter also needed to examine her
part of the problem. But years later, the mom still goes back
to that appointment as a turning point in her life. Her

daughter reflected back her own sin and insecurities. She acted as a mirror. Thankfully, this mom had the courage to view her daughter as a mirror of dangerous grace.

To walk through the back door of an adolescent's heart isn't just about our adolescents. *It's also about us.* We hope this chapter will encourage you to examine the mirrors of dangerous grace in your own house. The mirrors in our homes—those of our spouses and children—are often those mirrors that show us with the most truthfulness. They don't hide anything. This is the very reason they are mirrors of dangerous grace. The grace they offer carries with it a tremendous amount of power. In them, you will learn a great deal both about who you really are and the impact you have on your children.

Melissa recently asked a group of adults with grown children, "What do you wish you had known as a parent?" One of the men in the group quickly answered, "Impact. I had no idea how much I impacted my children. I had no idea that what I did and said had so much power."

As adults, we can choose to look into these adolescent mirrors or we can simply turn away. Unfortunately, a lot of us choose to do the latter. In the midst of a relatively calm discussion about his son's weekend plans, a father we know told his 17-year-old son, "You are ruining my life." This father is completely unaware of his impact. He is choosing not to examine his own life, ignoring both his son as a mirror and what he is mirroring to his son. If he were aware of his own foolish reflection or the sadness reflected in his son's eyes, he would never make such a statement.

The Adolescent Mirror

Why do you look at the speck that is in your brother's eye, but do not notice the log that is in your own eye? Or how can you say to your

brother, "Let me take the speck out of your eye,"
and behold, the log is in your own eye? You hyp-
ocrite, first take the log out of your own eye; and
then you will see clearly to take the speck out of
your brother's eye.

—MATTHEW 7:3-5 NASB

Without using a mirror, have you ever tried to remove an eyelash that has gotten in your eye? It is next to impossible. To remove an eyelash—much less a log—from our own eye, we must first be able to see it. Our adolescent children often provide us with the means to do so. They act as a mirror for us, reflecting back many things. For some reason, these adolescent mirrors seem to be particularly perceptive. They reach into the deepest, most hidden parts of who we are, revealing our fears, our insecurities, our dreams, and our sins.

Our Fears

Most children are not born afraid. They learn the concept of fear either by experience (something happening to them) or by example. A five-year-old child might be fascinated by snakes. But if, when walking in the park, he and his mom stumble across a snake and she screams, grabs him, and runs away, he has learned that snakes are to be feared.

The passing on of our fears usually goes unnoticed by the adult. We may even think our children have not caught on that we are afraid. But children are very perceptive mirrors. Cindy Morgan, a dear friend of ours who is an incredibly gifted songwriter, singer, and author, wrote a moving and inspiring book on the subject of fear, in which she candidly talks about the fear that has plagued her own life and its origins.

> When I think about the women in my family, I
> am inclined to believe that my struggle with fear
> is part of my family heritage. I feel the jangle of
> the chains of fear that have haunted these gen-
> erations of women in my family. I see the reflec-
> tion of those fears in my own eyes.[2]

In her book, Cindy describes the fears that plagued her throughout adolescence and early adulthood, and her journey toward freedom. She was and continues to be, through her writing, a mirror reflecting back the fear experienced by the women in her family.

Most of us who struggle with fears can look back in our family heritage and come to the same conclusion as Cindy. The fear has been passed on.

A woman who started her own high-profile business spoke with us recently about her fears. "I spend so much of my time trying to look good. It's like everyone else has this picture of me that I know isn't really me. But instead of being honest, I keep trying to live up to it. I live in constant fear that people will figure out what I'm really like." We asked her to tell us about her family and if anyone had ever talked to her about his or her own struggles with fear. "It's funny you should ask that because my mom and I had this talk the other day. My mother is a successful woman who has achieved a lot. She told me she was afraid of being "found out." She is afraid that the person she is inside is not the person that other people like and think she is. When she said those words, I thought 'That's it! That's exactly what I'm afraid of, too.'"

The fear may be of being found out, of snakes, of darkness, or of being alone. Whatever form our fears take, they will most likely be reflected in the lives of our adolescents. We can, however, do something to end this negative legacy. As we look into our adolescent mirrors, we can examine and confront our fears in a way that brings freedom, not only for ourselves, but also for our children.

Our Insecurities

As adults, many of us have walked through a crowd of teenagers and felt a tingling uncertainty. Simply spending time with adolescents can remind us of our own insecurities at their age. A few years ago, Melissa met with a youth director who felt he had lost control of his youth group. He described a group of five high school boys who had become involved in the group. These boys were attractive, confident, and a little rough around the edges. Other kids were drawn to them and, at the same time, intimidated by them. The youth leader was thrilled to have them involved in the church. He felt that he and his group had something to offer them. The more he got to know them, however, the more he felt himself succumbing to their intimidation. "I feel like an adolescent myself when I'm around them. I make stupid jokes, I lose my awareness of the other kids, and I think I just end up trying to impress them," he said.

The more this young man talked, the more he seemed to be drawn back into his own high school experience. He had been very intelligent, slightly overweight, involved in the band and in his own youth group. He had not, however, been accepted by the guys he considered "cool" at his school. In the midst of trying to minister to these adolescent boys, they had become mirrors of his own unresolved insecurities. He saw in them the friends he always wanted. He felt a sense of wanting to belong to their group and lost his sense of purpose in his job.

As parents, we often see the insecurities reflected in different ways. Gender appears to contribute to a parent's insecurities with their adolescent children. Adolescent daughters bring to light the insecurities of their mothers, and adolescent sons the insecurities of their fathers. Several years ago, a father spoke to Melissa about his fear of having a son. "It is so frightening to me to have a boy. I don't know how to work on motors, and I'm not good at fixing things around the house. I'm afraid I won't be able to teach him the things he needs to know." Just the thought of having a son brought out this man's insecurities about the things he felt he was supposed to be able to do as a man.

For women, the insecurity can turn into a critical view of their daughters. Mothers often see their daughters as extensions of themselves. They expect their daughters to be a perfected version of themselves. At the same time, a mother can dote on her son and have tremendous, unattainable expectations of her daughter without even realizing it.

Our Dreams

We spoke with parents recently whose son was the target of teasing on the school bus. The dad echoed what many of us feel when the children we love are hurting. "I wanted to get on that bus myself the next morning and tell those kids a thing or two," he said. To put it simply, we want good things for our kids. We want them to be loved, to feel confident, to feel significant. And we want them to have all the opportunities we didn't.

We talk to parents every day who want good things for their adolescent children. And we often talk to adolescent children who feel that the good things their parents want can put pressure on them.

- "My mom just won't let me quit cheerleading. I hate it. I'm embarrassed. But she tried out in high school and didn't make it. Now she thinks I'm wasting my talents if I don't do it."

- "I am tired of playing baseball. The coach pushes me way too hard. My dad wants me to go out with him every day and practice my pitching. He played baseball in college and would have made it to the major leagues if he hadn't blown out his arm. He says that if I keep it up, the scouts will be really impressed. I just want a normal life. I want to hang out with my friends after school. I like baseball, but I don't really care if I play again after high school. But just because I've had my name in the paper a few times, my dad says that God wants me to be a baseball player. I'm just not sure. I don't feel like God's told me what I'm supposed to do yet. It seems weird He'd tell my dad first."

Both of these adolescents are in the midst of the development we discussed in Chapter 1. They are just beginning to discover who they are and what they want. Both of these parents see what they believe to be extraordinary gifts God has given their children. They want good things for them...good things they wish they had been able to enjoy when they were younger. But these good things have led to pressure. And these perceptive adolescent mirrors are doing their best to reflect that to their parents. The problem is that the unfulfilled dreams of their parents are temporarily blocking the reflection.

Our Sins

Little Rock, Arkansas, was not the ideal place to be living as an adolescent in 1957. The public school system shut down, and all the students had to enroll in other school districts due to what is now known as the Crisis of Central High, which took place over the process of racial integration. Members of the National Guard stood post as nine students began the integration process in Arkansas public schools. White teenagers lined up on either side of the walkway hurling insults, among other things, as the new students were ushered into Little Rock Central High School. These white students were most likely acting as adolescent mirrors for their parents' attitudes. Many were reflecting the racial hatred that had been the fragrance of each of their homes that fall morning. They were speaking their parents' words and wearing their parents' expressions as they humiliated the African-American students who were courageously entering the school.

Not only do adolescents reflect our fears, insecurities, and dreams, they also very accurately reflect our sin. In his book *See You at the House*, Bob Benson told a story of just such mirrors (actually, an entire house of mirrors).

> I read about a man who said that he never fussed at an employee in the afternoon because he liked dogs. He went on to explain that usually what happened was that the man went home frustrated and fuming and the first thing he did was to give his wife a few short answers and make her mad also. About that time the oldest son would innocently stroll through the kitchen and mom would give him a verbal blast. He would then seek out his sister and pass it on. In a little while the baby brother would come wandering in and the sister would tell him in no uncertain terms to let her things alone and stay out of her room. And the poor little brother, being low man on the totem pole, would start out into the yard and see the dog asleep on the back step so he would just kick the dog. So the employer didn't bawl people out in the afternoon because he liked dogs.[3]

Ephesians 6 and Colossians 3 contain very similar verses about how we are to treat our children and how our sin impacts them. Colossians 3:21 (NASB) says, "Fathers [parents in another translation], do not exasperate your children, so that they will not lose heart." When we exasperate our children, or as Eugene Peterson says in his translation, "come down too hard" on them, we cause them to lose heart. We crush their spirit, and they become discouraged. Our sin is reflected in their mirror.

In *Reliving the Passion,* Walter Wangerin talks at great length about his wife as a mirror. "My wife is such a mirror. When I have sinned against her, my sin appears in the suffering of her face. Her tears reflect with terrible accuracy my selfishness."[4] Just as Wangerin's wife reflects his sin and selfishness, so do our adolescents reflect ours. When we exasperate and sin against them, our sin will often appear in the suffering of their faces. Some adolescents, however, have found that their faces are not a safe place to display their feelings. They learn to express their suffering silently.

A young woman told us a story about her father, who often went into a rage when things went wrong—not over big things like getting a promotion, but over little things like the lawnmower not starting or the car making a strange noise. From time to time, he would send her on an errand to find something for him. She knew that if she couldn't find it, he would scream at her and fly into a terrific rage. Because she knew what could happen, it almost certainly would happen. She would go into such a panic over her father's anger that she couldn't remember where anything was. This happened time and time again. Her suffering over her father's sinful response took the form of panic.

Whereas many adolescents lose heart when confronted by the sins of their parents, other adolescents reflect their parents' sin by taking it on as their own. Several years ago, Sissy met with the mother of an adolescent daughter who had become sexually promiscuous. Her mother caught her acting out with boys several times and was distraught. Over the course of their discussion, it came out that the mother was having her boyfriend spend the night at their house when the daughter was home. "We close the door and it's really none of her business. After all, it's different when you're an adult." This adolescent was functioning as a perceptive mirror, reflecting back the sins of her mother.

We have a choice in how we respond to our adolescent mirrors. We can pretend the reflection isn't there. We can simply turn away. Or we can use the mirrors as an opportunity for purging and renewal, as Wangerin suggested in the quote at the beginning of this chapter.

In our desire to be strong, loving, good parents or youth leaders, it is easy to get caught in a cycle of trying so hard that exhaustion sets in. Here you are driving to every type of practice imaginable, trying to provide your children with all the right things, and giving consequences when appropriate, and we are suggesting that you need to look in the mirror. It's enough to make you want to throw up your hands in frustration. As one parent of an adolescent said, "I don't have the luxury of looking at my life right now. I'm too busy trying to make my kids' lives good." Exactly. We try to be perfect parents, and then our kids mirror back to us our failures. We become frustrated and exhausted. But we are missing the point. God does not expect us to be perfect parents, but parents who experience the joy of forgiveness and the hope of healing.

We have heard countless times from kids how meaningful it is when a parent asks for forgiveness. Our adolescents are mirrors of dangerous grace. We will fail them. But in our failures, we have a choice. We can turn away from their reflection, or we can examine our own fears, insecurities, dreams, and sins. If we do, we can experience the purging, renewal, forgiveness, and healing that come through the Spirit of God and His Word. But to experience these things places us directly in front of the mirror.

*Do not merely listen to the word, and so deceive
yourselves. Do what it says. Anyone who listens
to the word but does not do what it says is like a
man who looks at his face in a mirror and, after
looking at himself, goes away and immediately
forgets what he looks like.*

—JAMES 1:22-24

We do have a choice. And whatever choice we make
determines the type of mirror we become in the lives of our
adolescents. When we give up the quest of perfect parenting and remove the logs from our own eyes, we become
much clearer mirrors ourselves.

The Adult Mirror

As adults, we have so much we want to reflect to our
children, both about who they are and who Christ is. Adolescents are not only mirrors for us, but we also act as mirrors for them. If we respond to our adolescent mirrors by
turning away from them, we will end up with cloudy mirrors ourselves. We will miss out on an opportunity for
purging and renewal. And our mirrors will not provide an
accurate reflection.

We have all been to an amusement park and looked at
the mirrors in the fun house. They are curved and bent in
a way that makes the person looking into them appear
shorter, heavier, or oddly distorted. Most of us who have
looked into these mirrors have pointed to our own reflections and laughed. We laugh because we know we are not
curved, or shorter, or heavier. We laugh because we know
we can walk away with confidence in who we really are.

When we are not taking the time to examine and deal
with our own lives, we become fun-house mirrors for our
adolescents. They will look into our mirrors and see themselves distorted and disfigured. Unfortunately, they do not

point and laugh. They believe that who they really are is what they see reflected in our mirrors, distorted or not.

A woman who is now in her 30s told us a story that was one of her most prominent memories of her grandmother. When she was about 11 years old, her grandmother was in the bathroom with her teaching her to shave her legs. The young girl was thrilled to be learning something she considered so grown-up, but then her grandmother turned to her and said, "You are so different than you used to be. You were much nicer when you were a little girl."

This grandmother was a fun-house mirror. She offered her granddaughter a reflection that was distorted. The grandmother could have seen this time as a rite of passage with her granddaughter. She could have helped her granddaughter see that she was becoming a woman of God with tremendous value. Instead, she made her granddaughter feel like something was wrong with her. The reflection was not only distorted, it was wrong. Because she did not understand the changes taking place in adolescence, this grandmother reflected to her granddaughter an image that the granddaughter was less than she had been, rather than helping her to become something more. The reflection was more a picture of the grandmother's own cloudy mirror than a reflection of the heart of this child.

There are two types of mirrors we can be as adults that will have a positive impact on the lives of our adolescents: mirrors that delight and mirrors that have purpose. A mirror that does both will give an accurate reflection of the value of our children.

A Mirror That Delights

Over the course of one week, we asked approximately 100 adolescents if they felt enjoyed by their parents. A few said, "Definitely." A few more said, "No way." And an overwhelming majority said things that sounded more like:

- "Well, I know my parents love me. I don't understand what you mean by 'enjoy.'"
- "I don't really know."
- "Maybe."
- "I'm not sure."

One girl who answered yes told us a story. She and her mom were in the grocery store late one night. One of their favorite songs came on the radio, and they just happened to be on separate ends of the cereal aisle. The mom immediately started singing the song and dancing down the aisle toward her daughter. The daughter joined in the chorus as they danced and sang all the way to the checkout line. This memory has stayed with this young girl because it was a time she felt enjoyed and delighted in by her mom.

One of the boys talked about a time he and his dad went to a father/son basketball camp together. "It was fun being with my dad away from home and the rest of our family. I got him all to myself."

Melissa remembers feeling enjoyed by her mom each time it snowed. Whatever hour of night, her mom would come into her room and wake her up. Together they would go to the window and watch the snow fall. Each time this happened, she felt her mother's delight in her. Melissa and her mom still call each other any time the snow begins to fall in Nashville or Kentucky, where Melissa's mom lives.

Unfortunately, many adolescents do not feel delighted in by their parents. And often, if they do, it is either because the parent has become the adolescent's buddy, or because the adolescent has achieved something significant.

The "buddy parent" is similar to the "dove parent" we talked about in the introduction. We are not, in any way, trying to support "buddy" parenting. Walter Wangerin makes this point in his book, *Little Lamb, Who Made Thee?* "Parents are not appointed to be the buddies of their children, seeking their affections and praise, seeking ever and ever to keep the kid happy. "

We can delight in our children and not feel that we have to be their best friend or keep them constantly happy. Even if we tried, because of the developmental shifts we talked about in Chapter 1, we would never be able to do so.

Delighting in our children's achievements is a good thing. To score the winning touchdown or get the lead in the school play is something to be celebrated for every adolescent. But there is a marked difference between delighting in our children's achievements and delighting in our children. To only delight in their achievements leaves them feeling that they either have to continue to achieve or that they are only delightful when they do.

Both of us lost a very dear friend to breast cancer last year. She was a strong, loving, warm woman with three children. Donna was a parent who would give consequences and tell the truth to her children, no matter how hard it was for them to hear. Just like every other parent, however, she was not perfect. But what she did for her children more than anything else was delight in them. Those children knew beyond a shadow of a doubt that they were loved and enjoyed by their mom, and they still do. Now they are becoming parents who delight in their own children.

Many children who are delighted in will begin to feel delightful. The parents are reflecting their enjoyment of the child, and the child begins to see that reflection as who they are. Sissy's mom has talked a great deal about something recommended by a well-known doctor in a book she read during her pregnancy with Sissy. He wrote at length about the importance of smiling at your children. Sissy's mom took that to heart and started smiling at both of her daughters the instant they came out of the womb (actually, as soon as she recovered enough to feel like smiling). Sissy and Kathleen, her sister, are 16 years apart. During their growing-up years, their parents have heard over and over that both their daughters seemed to smile all the time.

These examples are not intended as a grocery list of things to do to make your child feel delighted in. Delighting in our children is not about being their buddy or providing a constant vaudeville show to entertain them. Singing in the grocery, going with them to basketball camps, or waking them up for snow will not work for every adolescent. The answer is not found in what we do to enjoy our children. Once again, the answer comes in the kind of mirror we are.

As Eugene Peterson writes in his translation of Proverbs 27:19, "Just as water mirrors your face, so your face mirrors your heart" (*THE MESSAGE*).

When we are feeling delight in our children, our faces and our actions will register that delight. Our hearts are where it all begins. Our passion and enjoyment reside in our hearts, as does our sense of purpose. We will be discussing this in the next chapter.

A Mirror That Has Purpose

Hook was a movie that came out in the late '80s as a kind of sequel to the Disney classic *Peter Pan*. In it, Peter Pan denies the boyhood he once cherished. He has become Peter Panning: entrepreneur, workaholic, husband to Wendy's granddaughter, father of two children, and all-around bore. Peter Panning is everything he was not as Peter Pan. Needless to say, his kids do not feel enjoyed by him, or even really known by him. He treats them as more of a nuisance than anything else.

The plot develops as Captain Hook visits Wendy's home in England to kidnap Peter's two children. He leaves a note that challenges Peter to a fight to win the children back. A great deal of the movie takes place as Peter regains his identity as Peter Pan, along with his imagination and strength. He remembers his purpose.

The movie climaxes as the children are about to be killed by Captain Hook. Peter swoops in, green hat and all, to fight Hook and win back his children. His daughter, caught in the arms of Hook's men, looks up and delightedly exclaims, "Peter Pan's my dad!"

His daughter's excitement over her dad's newfound purpose is evident. She is proud of him, and proud to be Peter Pan's daughter. She feels secure and loved in his purpose.

A 13-year-old girl and her mother came in for their first appointment. The daughter had been diagnosed with depression, and the mother was beside herself with worry.

"I just don't know what to do for her. She is down all the time. I can't make her laugh anymore or even smile." The mother of this teenage girl was very rightfully worried. And she was doing her best to delight in her daughter, even in the midst of the depression. The daughter's story, however, took on an entirely different perspective.

"My mom won't quit hovering. She asks me how I'm doing all the time. She follows me to my room trying to talk to me. I feel like she would breathe for me if she could."

Because of her concern over her daughter, the mother had made this young girl the center of her world. This is very understandable. The child, however, felt *too* important. She felt trapped and consumed by her mother's worry. She no longer felt the delight her mother was desperately trying to communicate.

In our offices, we see this scenario quite often. The children are different ages and have different situations, but the result is the same. If a parent *only* mirrors delight to his child, the child begins to feel too important. After all, adolescents already believe they are the center of the universe. It is a step in the journey of their development. But to set up camp in the center of the universe can become a scary thing.

We have all seen signs and cross-stitched pillows labeled with the words, "The best thing a father can do for his children is to love their mother." This is true for many reasons. Obviously, it is best for children to grow up with both parents in the home. (We could write an entire book on that subject, but there is already a terrific one entitled *The Unexpected Legacy of Divorce*.)

For a father to love a child's mother also establishes the child's place in the scheme of things. It emphasizes that the child is not the cornerstone of their family. *The father has purpose beyond parenting.* Parenting may be part of his purpose, but it is not the only one. Of course, this principle applies to mothers, as well.

Many of us have been in grocery stores or malls and watched a toddler throwing a fit over something he wants. We have also seen the mother scramble to give him whatever he is screaming over. This child is learning the lesson that he gets whatever he wants.

The same thing can happen with adolescents. To be the center of the universe carries with it a number of demands. If our primary goal as parents is to make life work for our children, they will begin to see that as our job. They will believe that it is our fault when life doesn't work.

They also can become insecure under the weight of their parent's happiness. When a child is the apple of a parent's eye, they will sometimes feel that it is their job to stay there. They know, deep inside, that they can't keep their parent happy, but they will do their best to try. These children become more like adults than the teenagers they actually are.

It is important that children, and adolescents particularly, begin to understand what the world is really like. We are not saying that they have to go without food to understand hunger or to sleep outside to appreciate shelter. But we are saying that life is not always going to turn out the way they expect. And we are saying that they need to learn how to care for others...to give something of themselves for someone else. This is not at all natural for adolescents, or for any of us for that matter. But when they see this purpose mirrored by us, they begin to understand its importance.

It is easy for parents to give up things they are passionate about when their children are first born. To find the time for community work when you have an infant may feel impossible. Or who can paint when their child is toddling everywhere and getting into everything? It may be hard to find time to be with friends in the midst of soccer practices and cheering at basketball games. It can feel like the most difficult thing in the world to balance a job with parenting. Yet it is of vital importance that at least some of these things happen.

An adolescent told us recently that her mom goes on a reading retreat with her friends each year. "I'm glad she goes. She usually comes back happier and more relaxed."

This mom is mirroring purpose. She is mirroring to her teenage daughter that she is not the center of the universe. To volunteer, to paint, to spend time with friends, and to work can feel selfish for a parent. What these things actually do is to help prevent selfishness in your adolescent...especially when they are combined with delight.

To only delight in a child makes them feel too important. To only have purpose can make them feel discarded.

But to mirror both delight and purpose will help to make a child feel secure and loved, just like Peter Pan's daughter.

The Perfect Mirror

We love because he first loved us.

—1 JOHN 4:19

Jesus loved us by going to the cross and taking our sin upon Him as He was crucified. "We love because he first loved us."

> But God demonstrates his own love for us in this: While we were still sinners, Christ died for us.
>
> —ROMANS 5:8

"We love because he first loved us." And we are mirrors because He was first a mirror for us. Jesus was an adult mirror because He delighted in us and had unparalleled purpose. He was also an adolescent mirror that reflected all our fears, dreams, insecurities, and sins as He hung upon the cross. He was both of these mirrors, offering to us purging and renewal. But, He was different. He was the perfect mirror. *He was and is the mirror of dangerous grace.*

It takes courage to look into a perfect mirror. We see our sin, our selfishness, and our failure. We go to the cross and look into the face of Christ and see ourselves. That's the dangerous part.

But it is only when we have the courage to go to the cross and see our sin in the suffering of His face that we are able to hear His words, *"It is finished."*

These are the words of dangerous grace. When Christ said these words, the veil that separated man from God was lifted.

> *But we all, with unveiled face, beholding as in a*
> *mirror the glory of the Lord, are being trans-*
> *formed into the same image from glory to glory,*
> *just as from the Lord, the Spirit.*
>
> —2 CORINTHIANS 3:18 NASB

This is where it leads for all of us. We look into the mirror of Christ and see our sin. But because the veil has been lifted, we are being transformed. That is hope. And that is the true mirror of dangerous grace.

A 12-year-old boy was getting ice cream with Melissa and a group of boys his age at Daystar. With blue ice cream all over his face, he smiled and quietly said, "I accepted Christ again. I saw the cross and it was awful. And He did that for me."

As parents, counselors, teachers, youth directors, and anyone else who loves adolescents, what we ultimately want to reflect is Christ. We want to be mirrors that reflect His purging, renewal, delight, and purpose. We want to offer our children the love that has first been given to us.

3
Sound Tracks

> To live without listening at all is to live deaf to the
> fullness of the music. Sometimes we avoid listening
> for fear of what we may hear, sometimes for fear that
> we may hear nothing at all but the empty rattle of
> our own feet on the pavement. Listen for him. Listen
> to the sweet and bitter airs of your present and your
> past for the sound of him.[1]
>
> —FREDERICK BUECHNER, LISTENING TO YOUR LIFE

One of our favorite sound tracks of all time is from the movie *Simon Birch*. The songs range from moving instrumentals to R&B classics by artists such as Marvin Gaye and Smokey Robinson. Melissa bought it immediately after she saw the movie. The music, however, loses something significant when it is simply fed through a stereo system. It loses something of its power. The poignancy of the soundtrack has much to do with the relationship of the songs to the scenes from the movie.

The Christmas pageant scene is one of the most memorable moments from *Simon Birch*. Because of a birth defect that profoundly stunted his growth, Simon is cast in the role of the baby Jesus. The girl he has a crush on is cast as Mary. Although he is small, Simon is experiencing the plagues of adolescence in full swing. During the program, Mary bends over to touch Jesus lying in the manger, and

Simon catches sight of Mary partially exposed. As his face begins to register what he has seen, we hear the stirrings of Peggy Lee's "Fever" in the background. It is the perfect song at the perfect time.

Sound tracks are the music that brings movies to life, used to accentuate and draw out the emotional significance of what is taking place in a particular scene. What would *Jaws* be without the haunting, simple melody that always accompanies the shark's explosion onto the screen? Darth Vader wouldn't be nearly so ominous and the dinosaurs from *Jurassic Park* wouldn't strike such terror into our hearts without their respective musical themes. We'll never forget the songs from movies such as *Brian's Song* and *On Golden Pond* for the same reason. We are stirred emotionally by the images on screen, but our hearts are freed to move by the music.

The Sound Track of Home

Melissa often has a sound track taking place in her lake house, called Hopetown, where we have our Daystar summer camps. At any given moment, the sound track might be squeals of laughter from the eighth-grade girls upstairs on the sleeping porch or the cheering of boys as they watch one of their friends learn how to water-ski. And every night, you can hear the enthusiastic singing and clapping as we sing songs like "I Go to the Rock." This sound track always moves Melissa's sheepdog, Molasses. Whenever she hears cheering, singing, or laughter, Molasses comes to life. She runs to the person making the noise and barks and barks until they stop.

As sound tracks bring life to movies, and the sounds of Melissa's home bring life to Molasses, so as adults, our lives can have the same impact on the adolescents we love. *Our lives and the way we relate to our children provide the sound track of our homes.*

Each home has its own sound track. Each adult who is in relationship with an adolescent provides a sound track that creates the backdrop for that relationship. Think back over different scenes with your adolescent. What was the accompanying music? Was it loud or soft? Peaceful or chaotic? Sad or excited? Encouraging or critical?

Rosie O'Donnell tells a story about a woman who profoundly impacted her during her own adolescence. Pat Maravel was Rosie's eighth-grade math teacher and a woman she affectionately called "Teach."

> I am not sure when it began, my list making, but by the time I was in eighth grade it was routine. Every night as I fell off to dreamland, I would count them off, out loud, in a hushed whisper— my dad, brothers, sister and nana, those close enough to ruin me should they up and die. There were six of them. Six was manageable, six was unavoidable. I pictured them as I dozed off, in the red bull's-eye of my heart, unaware of their power, or their place in the danger zone. One night I saw her, Teach, sitting there next to my family, inside my inner circle. Wanted, needed, loved. I stopped talking to her the next day. I ignored her. I would not respond to anything she said or did. She thought it was a game and tried to make me laugh. I was a hard sell. To her credit, she did not give up or turn away. She came after me full force. She baited me, stopping me in the hall, telling me jokes. She wrote witty remarks in the margins of my tests.[2]

Pat formed the sound track for many years of Rosie's life. She did not give up, even when Rosie's fear may have made it difficult to care for her. The sound track Pat provided was one of stability, surprise, and love. As adolescents will do, Rosie opened up the back door of her heart and allowed Pat to walk right in.

We all have sound tracks that helped form our lives. We all had parents, teachers, youth directors, and others who provided these sound tracks. But we may not have all been as fortunate as Rosie was in having Pat. Some of our sound tracks may have been more destructive than affirming. In either case, these sound tracks formed more than just our individual lives. They also helped form the life of our relationships. *The sound tracks of our pasts and the sound tracks that we are hearing now significantly impact our relationships with the adolescents we love.*

What We Heard

What was the sound track like in your own home growing up? In your school? In your youth group? Hopefully, in one of those places or another, you had an experience with people who affirmed and helped shape your life in a positive way.

Unfortunately, the experiences we remember more often are the destructive ones. Wade Boggs expressed this well after his team, the Boston Red Sox, lost the World Series. As he was interviewed in the midst of the winning team's hoopla, he simply said, "Losing hurts worse than winning feels good." Many times, our most significant memories are the ones that involve pain. They are memories of being laughed at, betrayed, and abandoned.

Every one of us can look back on our lives and see these moments of pain. Whether through death or divorce, betrayal or loss, we all have been touched by sorrow in one form or another, often at the hand of someone loved and trusted.

As adults, it is important to remember what we have heard. In the quote that opens this chapter, Frederick Buechner reminds us to listen to our present and past for the voice of God. It is often in the most painful places that we can find God, or that He can find us. Eugene Peterson translates 2 Corinthians 12:7 this way: "Satan's angel did his best to get me down; what he in fact did was push me to my knees" (*THE MESSAGE*).

We see this on a daily basis in our offices. We see parents and kids who have walked through tremendous suffering and found hope as a result of their painful experience. One adolescent boy we worked with had to be hospitalized for his depression. His response surprised us. "I'm really glad I went," he said. "I'm not sure how, but I found God again while I was in the hospital. I didn't want to go. But I think if I hadn't gone I would still be where I was. I would still be lost." He saw specifically how God was redeeming his pain. Dan Allender, in his book *The Healing Path*, talks about how God uses pain to bring about His redemption.

> Many people I know bear stories with so much tragedy and horror that I have privately wondered how they have chosen to live another day. But what I have most often noted as I've listened to these people is their determined passion to embrace life. Although some people allow their hurts to make them bitter, I am amazed by the many who have suffered profoundly yet sing with both the deepest strains of sorrow and the most haunting melodies of hope.[3]

It is not unusual for parents to talk about wanting to raise their children differently than they were raised.

- "My parents were very legalistic and judgmental. I don't want to be that way with my child."

- "I had an abusive father. I want to learn how to discipline my son and remind him that I believe in him at the same time."

- "My mother was around. But I don't have one memory of her ever being kind to me. I want to be a good mom. I'm just not sure I know how."

Each of these statements is loaded with pain. In response to that pain, each of these parents has been pushed to their knees in their need for Christ. They want their pasts to be redeemed through the lives of their own adolescents. What Satan tries to use to destroy us, God can use to create sound tracks that are even more powerful in the lives of our adolescents. To listen to our past reminds us of God's redemption, and it can give birth to music inside of us that draws others to Christ.

What We Hear

Each of us has grown up with our own sound tracks. In fact, we have a sound track playing right now, one that no one else can hear...the sound track in our minds. Anne Lamott, in her book *Bird by Bird*, uses the metaphor of a radio station that plays mercilessly in the mind of writers. (For those of you who read and enjoy Anne Lamott like we do, you'll notice that we have softened her style just a bit by leaving out a few words.)

> If you are not careful, station____ will play in your head twenty-four hours a day, nonstop, in stereo. Out of the right speaker in your inner ear will come the endless stream of self-aggrandizement, the recitation of one's specialness, of how much more open and gifted and brilliant and knowing and misunderstood and humble one is. Out of the left speaker will be the rap songs of self-loathing, the lists of all the things one

doesn't do well, of all the mistakes one has made today and over an entire lifetime, the doubt, the assertion that everything that one touches turns to [poop], that one doesn't do relationships well, that one is in every way a fraud, incapable of selfless love, that one has no talent or insight, and on and on and on.[4]

We talk to ourselves about ourselves continuously. As Anne Lamott notes, we are usually either hearing our own self-adulation from the right speaker of our minds or the degrading of ourselves from the left speaker. Many times, these thoughts are filtered through what we have heard about ourselves while growing up.

As parents or those in relationships with adolescents, our thoughts probably contain sentences such as these:

- "I can't believe he talks to me this way when I drive him everywhere he wants to go. All I ever do is sit behind that wheel. I feel more like a taxi driver than a dad."

- "She doesn't know how lucky she is. Most mothers would never take the time to homeschool their kids."

- "She says she wants to spend more time with me. I'm home when she gets home from school, and we talk then. I just need to be able to have time with my friends in the evenings. I know this divorce has been hard on her, but I need to do what helps me heal."

The right speaker keeps us in the role of a martyr. We concentrate more on our own needs and feelings than those of our children. It's important that we are aware of what's happening inside of us. Surely every parent will have these types of thoughts at one time or another. They are to be expected when we are dealing with adolescents who are by nature unresponsive and self-absorbed. But it becomes destructive to our relationships with our teens when these right-speaker sounds are the only sounds we hear.

The left-speaker thoughts can also create problems, in that they attack our self-confidence as parents. "I have never done anything right as a parent, my advice never seems to help them, they don't think I'm fun, they never want to spend time with me, they don't even like me, and so on." We could easily do this to ourselves 24 hours a day, seven days a week, and spiral down into a debilitating depression. If these are the only sounds we hear, they will most likely lead us to communicate the same type of sounds to our kids. It is difficult to hate yourself without at least part of the hate spilling over onto the people you love.

During our summer camps, Sissy plays the guitar and leads worship each night. She has played the guitar for years and led worship with the kids since joining the staff. Every once in a while, in the midst of worship, the "radio station voices" will start. "You can't play the guitar. And what do you think you're doing trying to sing? You don't sing half as well as Celia, and Justin plays the guitar a million times better. You need to just sit down." From there, it's just like snow skiing. Once the thought pops into your head that you can't do it, all you seem able to do is to fall. If you give in, the "voice" can be paralyzing.

It feels impossible to lead others into truth when all you can hear is your own self-deprecating voice. Of course, it is equally impossible to love your children if you are consumed by the grandeur of your own parenting. In his book *Living the Message*, Eugene Peterson speaks of a similar conflict and advises us to respond in this way:

> The primary way in which we counter our stubborn propensities…is by cultivating humility. Learning to be just ourselves, keeping close to the ground, practicing the human, getting our

fingers in the humus, the rich, loamy, garden dirt out of which we have been fashioned. And then listen.[5]

The cacophony of the right and left speakers combined prevents us from listening. They become all that we hear and, in turn, become what we communicate into the lives of the adolescents we love. *The combination of what we have heard and what we are hearing has everything to do with the kind of sound track we provide for our adolescents.*

The Sound Track of Silence

A mom and dad recently called our offices, frantic for an appointment. Their teenage daughter was completely out of control. The cell phone they had given her for safety had, instead, given her liberty. She would call to check in with them, say she was at the mall, and be somewhere else with the very kids they were trying to keep her from. They would tell her to come home, and she would refuse. She had just spent her third night in the juvenile detention center. They were not only panicked but in a state of total helplessness.

Your situation may not be as dramatic as that of these frustrated parents. It may simply be that the communication in your home has broken down. Whatever the scenario, when we love adolescents, our feelings of frustration, disappointment, rage, and helplessness are aroused. As Mike Mason wrote, "Is it really so strange if your teenagers have a unique ability to arouse your rage and confront you with helplessness? This is their job."[6] It is also part of their developmental makeup.

As those who love adolescents, we do our best to be prepared for the tumultuousness of their teenage years. We read every book we can find on the subject. We take parenting classes. We think we know what is awaiting us as they move through puberty and into adolescence. We try to have a sound track that is not only affirming, but perfect. And then it hits. Our knowledge flies out the window in the face of their moodiness. We have no idea how to respond to their defiance. We feel helpless. And we are silenced in the face of the helplessness.

Thanks be to God.

Consider these two translations of Romans 10:17. "Before you trust, you have to listen" (THE MESSAGE). "So faith comes from hearing, and hearing by the word of Christ" (NASB).

Many times, this silence is precisely what God has been waiting for. It is only when we are silent that we are finally able to hear His voice. The deafening noises of our present and past then fade into the background. The silence opens us up to new sounds and deeper truth than we have heard before. In her novel *Death Comes for the Archbishop*, Willa Cather describes the experience that can come out of the silence.

> The Miracles of the Church seem to me to rest not so much upon faces or voices or healing power coming suddenly near to us from afar off, but upon our perceptions being made finer, so that for a moment our eyes can see and our ears can hear what there is about us always.[7]

How do we see that which is "about us always"? How do we allow our pasts to drive us to our knees in our need for Christ? How do we learn to hear His voice in the present rather than our own voices of despair and panic?

The answer lies in our dependence. We are silenced by our helplessness in loving our adolescents. *It is out of the silence that we hear and that we listen to His Word.*

From the very first day, we were there, taking it all in—we heard it with our own ears, saw it with our own eyes, verified it with our own hands. The Word of Life appeared right before our eyes; we saw it happen! And now we're telling you in most sober prose that what we witnessed was, incredibly, this: The infinite Life of God himself took shape before us.

We saw it, we heard it, and now we're telling you so you can experience it along with us, this experience of communion with the Father and his Son, Jesus Christ. Our motive for writing is simply this: We want you to enjoy this, too. Your joy will double our joy!

—1 John 1, The Message

Turning on the Sound Track

The silence can lead us to dependence, the dependence can cause us to listen, and the listening can lead us to joy. We, in turn, can lead our adolescents to the same place. We want the sound track of our home to be one of joy, of hope, and ultimately, of Christ.

Sound Tracks are the music that bring movies to life. We want our sound tracks to do the same thing for the adolescents we love. Now how do we go about doing this? We begin by listening. Hearing and listening are common themes throughout Scripture. In both the Hebrew and Greek translations, the words mean to *grasp the message and to respond to what has been said.*

We can listen to our past and present. We can allow ourselves to be silenced in our helplessness. But even then we may never actually respond in a way that brings life to our adolescent.

The way that we bring life to our adolescent is through our response. This response always occurs in the context of relationship. Isaiah 50:4b says, "He awakens me morning by morning, He awakens my ear to listen as a disciple" (NASB). Response comes from knowing and understanding our teenagers and from examining our own lives to see that we are reflecting Christ to them instead of our own sins, fears, insecurities, or dreams.

In his book *Connecting*, Larry Crabb tells about an experience with his own son that was life changing for them both. His son had been expelled from college, and Larry was on his way to bring him home.

> I drove the hour and a half trip to Taylor through open fields of Indiana farmland on quiet country roads. God was near. I talked with him as if he were sitting in the passenger seat. "Lord, I've done everything I know to do. I've not reached my son. And I can't reach him now. I don't know how to do it. But I'm not asking for instructions. I'm asking you to let him see Christ in me. Nothing will change him but a taste of what his heart most deeply wants. Principles, insights, rebukes just won't do it. He needs to meet you. Give yourself to him through me, please![8]

Larry was silenced by his helplessness. In his silence, he reached out to God. The book goes on to tell of their reunion, from both of their perspectives.

Larry: "Something came out of me and reached the tender part of Kep's soul with healing power."

Kep: "I did come back to the Lord during that time, but first I came back to you."[9]

In that moment, God used Larry to provide his son with a sound track that significantly re-formed the life of his son.

As adults who love adolescents, we have the opportunity to live our lives and relate to them in a way that frees them to experience Christ.

God uses who we are and who we have been to give birth to a rich, passionate sound track. He uses our present helplessness to call us to greater dependence. He uses our past to remind us of His redeeming love. God weaves these two melodies together into a sound track that is richer than any we could possibly create on our own.

Backdoor Dancing

It may be difficult to imagine dancing to a sound track. But, we can assure you it is possible. We have a tradition of going to movies at the end of each Daystar summer camp with our staff. Several summers ago, we saw *An Ideal Husband*. We loved the movie and were swept up in the Victorian irony of it. It also had a wonderful sound track that filled the theater as the credits rolled at the end of the film. Before we knew it Briana and Ben, two of our interns, were on the stage in front of the movie dancing with all their hearts to the music.

No one told Briana and Ben to go to the front of the theater. The music invited them, and they danced. When we are hearing God's voice, the sound track He creates through our present and past will flow through us to our adolescents. In the context of unpredictability and relationship, our sound tracks invite the adolescents we love to dance. Hopefully, we'll be able to dance with them...right through the back door of their hearts.

Part Two

Soften

Soften

At this point, we hope we have given you an idea of how to find the back door of your adolescent's heart. To walk through it requires both unpredictability and the connection of relationship. In Part One, we examined who adolescents are, what they want, and how they usually go about getting it. We took a hard look at what we reflect to our teens and what their reflections say about us. We also discussed the importance of our own sound tracks in the lives of our adolescents. What we listen to has a great deal to do with the kind of relationship we offer them. Most importantly, we hope you are hearing that it all goes back to Christ. When we look to Him as a model for relationship and listen to His truth, we invite our adolescents to be a part of something much richer than what we can offer on our own.

A friend of ours read one of the chapters in this section. Her first response was, "I wanted to talk to my daughter. I wanted to ask her what I am like as a mom."

She could not have said anything more encouraging. That is exactly what we want this book to do. Our hope, as you read, is that you will put the book down a lot. We would love for you to talk about these things with your adolescent. Share with them parts of the book that have piqued your interest. Ask them what they feel you reflect to them. Find out what they learn about themselves from you. Ask what kind of sound track they are hearing in your home. It will make for some meaningful and possibly difficult conversations. But it will also help you make your way through the back door of their hearts.

So, we're through the back door. What now? As adults, we walk (or dance) through the back door with them into relationship. This is the beginning of the process of reconnecting to the adolescents we love.

Softening is the first thing that takes place once the back door is open. Section Two will describe what softening looks like in the life of an adolescent. It's about creating a place where an adolescent can feel safe and free to be honest about their world and about themselves. It's also about reminding them that they are not alone, that as an adult, we enjoy and care about them deeply. In this section, we'll describe the importance of safety, simplicity, and enjoyment in relationship to our adolescents and in our own lives, as well.

4

In Here and Out There

———~———

It just feels like there's such a difference between in here and out there. Out there, my parents are getting a divorce. I hate my school because I don't fit in. I've lost most of my friends. In here, I don't know...it just feels safe and different.

—A HIGH SCHOOL STUDENT

In here and out there...we all have some variations on the difference between how it feels in here and out there. In here feels safe. Out there feels scary. In here, we feel loved. Out there, we're not really sure.

In here and out there are different for every one of us, and for every age. For Melissa, "in here" is being surrounded by people who care, who are passionate about the same things she's passionate about, and who want to talk about those things. For Sissy, "in here" involves those same people: people who she knows love and believe in her, but she is more likely to go to a movie with them or listen to music rather than just talk. We all find safety in different places.

Feeling safe as an adolescent is very different than it was when our teens were small children. A mom recently told Melissa that her daughter used to be terribly afraid of bugs. "All I had to do, when she saw a bug, was squash it. Now that she's becoming afraid of other things, I'm not really sure what to do. It doesn't feel like I can do anything."

The fears of children tend to be pretty simple. They are afraid of monsters or bugs, things we can either protect them from or help them realize don't actually exist. For adolescents, the fears are different. As we discussed in Chapter 1, their fears are becoming much more reality based. (Though Sissy still believes that the fear of bugs is definitely reality based!) Adolescents are afraid of being left out, being laughed at, or of looking like a fool. They are afraid of many of the same things that adults are. As much as we may want to, those of us who love them cannot protect them from these fears or tell them they don't exist. They do. And many times, we cannot stop the fears from becoming reality. *What we can do, however, is create safe places and invite our adolescents to experience them.*

In this chapter, we'll talk about what it means to *be* a safe place for your children. It involves offering them the freedom to wander, but a structure within that freedom. We'll also look at our own "safe places" and learn how to invite our adolescents to experience the kind of safety we have found.

Creating a Safe Place

We need to say at the outset that there is no perfectly safe place or safe person. None of us will be protected from all hurt and all pain until we get to heaven. And none of us will ever be able to completely stop causing hurt and pain to those we love until that time. Hopefully, we can give the teens we love a taste of safety, and a taste of what is to come.

Home Plate

In most children's games, we are "safe" when we arrive at a certain place, be it a tree or a base. In games, this place is considered "home." We may go out from home to risk and face danger, but we always have that one place to come back to. We all have seen the baseball player who leaves third base suddenly. The outfielder who has the ball throws it as fast as he can toward home plate. And right before the ball arrives, we hear the umpire yell, "SAFE!" At that moment, there is nowhere else that runner would rather be. To arrive there creates a feeling of relief.

That's what adolescents want. They want, and even need, to take risks. They need to stretch themselves and discover who they are. But they also long for a safe place to come back to.

During our summer camps, we played a game on the first morning of each camp. Everyone had to find someone they didn't know and ask that person three questions. These questions helped the kids learn something about each other, which they would then share with the group. One of the questions was, "Where is a place you feel safe?" You can imagine the different kind of answers we got, especially with the different age groups. Many kids said, "My safe place is at home." A few said that trees were their safe places; some said the beach. But one adolescent girl had an entirely different answer. "My safe place is my mom." We know this girl's mom. Deb is about as safe as a mom can be. We'll tell you why a little later on in this chapter.

We can be home for our adolescents, whether they actually live with us or not. To be home or to be safe for them means the same thing that home plate does in baseball. It means being present and available. Home plate does not move. For us to be home plate is for us to have that same kind of stability. Then our adolescents can be free to take risks and explore their world, knowing they can come back to us. We should encourage their independence, their growth in their own personal identity, and their ability to express what they personally feel. But they also need a home plate.

We talked earlier about the similarities between toddlers and adolescents. Toddlers will wander away from their parents, looking back every so often. An adolescent's journey to independence is very similar. Teenagers will wander and explore, but occasionally they will look back to make sure we are still present. They feel safe in that kind of freedom, having us as home plate.

A friend in college recently said this about her first week at school. "It has been hard, but really good. A few days ago, I had a time where I kind of fell apart. But God met me during that time. And He used my precious dad as I cried, and my voice shook over the phone. Sometimes you just need to cry, you know." This adolescent did need to cry. And she needed a safe place to do that. Her dad was safe for her. She had no question in her mind that she could pick up the phone and he would want to be there.

Of course, it is possible for us to be there to a fault. When we are safe for our adolescents in ways that do not encourage them to take risks, we do more harm than good.

An article in *Time* magazine said:

> It is a natural, primitive instinct to want to make your child happy and protect him from harm or pain. But that instinct, if not tempered, also comes with a cost. Adolescents can't learn to become emotionally resilient if they don't get any practice with frustration or failure inside their protective cocoons.[1]

An adolescent girl came for counseling several years ago because she was experiencing severe social anxiety. She never wanted to go to any kind of social function and was terrified at the thought of even spending the night at a friend's house. It would have been very easy for her mom to be content with being her only place of safety and not encourage her to take risks. But, her mom did encourage her. She told us a story that has stayed with us, because it is one that speaks powerfully of the heart of real safety.

> It was Friday night, and it was the first dance at her new high school. She did not want to go. She screamed and yelled and said she was absolutely not going. I told her she didn't have any choice and that we were leaving in ten minutes. Surprisingly, she got in the car, but proceeded to cry the whole way there. I didn't say a word, but drove up to the school and opened the door. She got out and walked into the building. Honestly, it broke my heart to have to do it. I hated to see her in that kind of pain. I did not want to make her go, but I knew she needed to. So, I circled around and parked my car in the school parking lot. I sat in my car the entire time she was at the dance and prayed for her.

Did her daughter emerge from the dance and say, "Oh, Mom, thanks for making me go. It was the best time I've ever had?" No. She came home and went straight to her room. But the mom's decision was not dependent on the response of her daughter. She wanted her daughter to learn that her fears do not have to control her. She wanted her to see that even in the midst of difficult things, she can take some risks and still have a safe place to come home to. And that is precisely what happened. Whether she ever admits it or not (and most adolescents probably won't), this young girl learned that she can take risks and still be loved. And her safe place will feel even safer because of the risk.

Structure

Several years ago, we were riding in the car with a friend named Staci. When we passed a billboard advertising invisible fences, Melissa looked up and said, "Why would you need a fence if it was invisible?" After we all laughed for a few minutes, Staci explained the purpose of invisible fences.

Invisible fences do not actually keep anything out, but they keep your dog from straying beyond the boundaries of your yard. Your dog is free to go wherever he likes as long as he doesn't attempt to leave the section that is fenced in. When he does, there are consequences.

Consequences are the invisible fences for our adolescents. While it is important that we give them safety and structure, they need to learn that there are consequences for their actions. But, as we have stated before and will talk about in later chapters, it is important that they have a choice.

A teenage boy at one of our summer camps several years ago told Melissa how things were changing around his house since he had gotten into trouble. (Trouble for this boy involved large amounts of drugs, alcohol, and stealing.) His parents were divorced, and his dad was a terrible influence on him.

> My mom has been really different lately. She is doing things like wanting to know where I am all of the time and when I'm coming home. My dad came to my birthday party last week and tried to give me marijuana for my birthday present. I told him I didn't want it because I knew it would make my mom really mad. It's weird that

> she's been so different. I don't really like it, but
> I'm glad, too.

This adolescent boy grinned the whole time he was telling his story. In the midst of the structure his mom was providing for him, he felt safe. Adolescents, again, want to be free to wander, but they also want parameters on their wandering. We need to offer them strength and compassion at the same time. The strength says that our parameters are still there, but the compassion reminds them that we are a safe place.

As children start to move into adolescence, they usually need fewer rules. They know now not to touch something hot, and they know to look both ways before crossing the street. Some parents have a hard time letting go of some of the rules of childhood. One of the things we say constantly to parents of adolescents is, "Choose your battles." The rules should be fewer, but you want the rules that are in place to be emphasized. At this age, kids have a tendency to tune us out when we say too much. Therefore, we encourage parents to set down fewer rules, but to enforce them with conviction!

The structure that most parents seem to emphasize has to do with things like curfews and car dates. We spend a lot of our time setting up parameters for how they should spend their time. These parameters are very important. They not only make our kids feel safe, but give them a sense of being grounded.

An article in *Time* magazine addressed what can happen when adolescents are not given parameters.

> Here is a parenting parable for our age. Carla
> Wagner, 17, of Coral Gables, Fla., spent the after-
> noon drinking the tequila she charged on her
> American Express Gold Card before speeding

off in her high-performance Audi A4. She was dialing her cell phone when she ran over Helen Marie Witty, a 16-year old honor student who was out rollerblading. Charged with drunken driving and manslaughter, Carla was given a trial date—at which point her parents asked the judge whether it would be O.K. if Carla went ahead and spent the summer in Paris, as she usually does.[2]

The article goes on to emphasize the need to provide structure for our children. They'll need some structure throughout their lives. But we can't keep them wrapped in a protective cocoon. At some point or another, they will have to learn to be responsible and that they can't always get their own way. In the short term, laying down the law may make life more difficult for us, but in the long run we'll make it easier for them to get along in life. This structure also makes them feel safe.

It is not just rules about their activities that are important for adolescents, but also rules about how they treat others. In the beginning of this chapter, we quoted a high school boy who talked about the difference between being "in here" and "out there." The "in here" he talked about was Daystar. We have several foundational, nonnegotiable rules at Daystar. These include calling people by name, not being sarcastic, and not making fun of people. Overall, we tell them our main rule is simply to be kind.

One of our middle school students told her mom, "The reason I like Daystar so much is because you're just not allowed to make fun of people." This rule is especially important to this adolescent. She is the girl we talked about before who went to sit with all of her friends at the lunch table, and they all got up and sat somewhere else. She has lived many years with being made fun of. She longs for and needs places where she feels safe.

We cannot say enough that there are no perfect places or perfect people. Daystar is included in that. We have failed many times and will fail again in the rules we have established. But the rules are there, and the kids know that there are consequences when they are broken.

Adolescents need structure. They need invisible fences that give them freedom to move but shock the fire out of them when they move too far. They need to be reminded of the importance of kindness and of respecting others. We all do. And they need to be reminded that they are not in charge. They will not tell you so themselves, but the world actually feels much safer for them that way.

Inviting Them to a Safe Place

Brennan Manning, in his book *Abba's Child*, asks the question, *"What is a safe place?"* He goes on to answer the question from an experience he writes about in his own journal.

> To feel safe is to stop living in my head and sink down into my heart and feel liked and accepted...not having to hide anymore and distract myself with books, television, movies, ice cream, shallow conversation...staying in the present moment and not escaping into the past or projecting into the future, alert and attentive to the now...feeling relaxed and not nervous or jittery...no need to impress or dazzle others or draw attention to myself...Unself-conscious, a new way of being with myself, a new way of being in the world...calm, unafraid, no anxiety about what's going to happen next...loved and valued...just being together as an end in itself.[3]

Hopefully, all of us have experienced these kind of safe places at one time or another. We have had places where we have felt loved, protected, and sheltered. It may have been with a group of people to whom we felt connected, it may have been in our own homes growing up, or it may even have been at a specific place geographically.

One of Sissy's safe places is Camp Waldemar, a picturesque camp nestled in the Texas hill country where she spent six summers while growing up. Sissy loved Waldemar, and still loves going to pick her sister up at the end of camp each summer. Because it is a place that has been safe and meaningful for her, it is something she wants to share. It just so happens that a good friend of ours named Gail went to Waldemar, too, and has had the same connection with the camp. For Sissy's birthday one year, Melissa, Sissy, Gail, and another close friend, Nita, flew down to Texas and spent a weekend at Waldemar. Because Gail and Sissy both felt safe at camp, it was a place they wanted to invite others to experience.

We are like that with our safe places. When we experience something so meaningful that it moves us deeply, we want to share that experience. It is a natural response. And when we, as adults who love adolescents, have tasted true safety, we want to invite them to the same experience.

Earlier, we mentioned Deb, a mom who is her daughter's safe place. We said that we know this mom, and we know why she is safe. Deb is a safe place for her daughter simply because she has experienced a safe place of her own. That safe place is Jesus. Deb has walked through hard times and found an anchor in the midst of them. Her life and heart have been changed as a result. The most natural response in the world is for her to invite her daughter to that same safe place.

> *...we who have fled to take hold of the hope offered to us may be greatly encouraged. We have*

this hope as an anchor for the soul, firm and secure. It enters the inner sanctuary behind the curtain, where Jesus, who went before us, has entered on our behalf.

—HEBREWS 6:18B-20A

We who have run for our very lives to God have every reason to grab the promised hope with both hands and never let go. It's an unbreakable spiritual lifeline, reaching past all appearances right to the very presence of God where Jesus, running on ahead of us, has taken up his permanent post as high priest for us....

—HEBREWS 6:18-20 THE MESSAGE

We love THE MESSAGE translation of this verse because it describes the motion we experience the most with adolescents. When an adolescent is part of your life, you seem to run a lot. Parents of adolescents don't sit and wait for hope, they run for it. And this very hope is an anchor for our soul, firm and secure...our safe place. William R. Newell, in his commentary on Hebrews, *Hebrews Verse by Verse*, talks about what happens to us as we take hold of this hope. He wrote, *"It is not our holding fast, but His holding fast to us."*[4]

It is not our holding on to Christ that brings us safety. For once we grab hold, He is the one holding fast to us. He is our safe place. We will go through difficulties, and we may run for our very lives. But we have One who has run on ahead of us to be our home plate. And that is something we can invite our adolescents to experience.

Several years ago, a mom came into our offices with her two adolescent boys. She said, "I don't have much time, so I want to get right down to it. I am a Christian, and I'm dying of AIDS."

This precious mom was literally running for her life to grab hold of Christ. In what would be her final year on earth, she found Christ to be her safe place. As she sat in Melissa's office, what was most important to her was that her sons find that same safety. She was inviting them, and she wanted other people in their lives who would echo that invitation after she was gone.

She died almost a year after she first brought her boys to Daystar. We have every confidence that she is finally, truly safe in heaven. Her boys have now both graduated from high school, and both have given their lives to Christ. She will see them again.

We have spoken of creating safe places for our children. We have talked about inviting them to the safe places we have found. How do the two tie together? They do in the same way they did for both of these moms. It happens in a cycle. These moms are not safe within themselves. Madeleine L'Engle, who found a safe place in her own parents, says it well in her book, *Walking on Water*.

> I trusted my parents, thank God, and I think that my children trust me. We all fail each other; none of us is totally trustworthy; but the more we are trusted, the more we become worthy of trust.[5]

If we want to be safe places for our children, we can give them freedom to wander and the parameters on that freedom that will help to make them feel safe. But we are the safest when we have experienced safety ourselves. *The more we feel safe, the more able we are to be safe for our children.*

In football, the safety is the defensive back in the deepest position. He stays in the background. He is usually not seen or noticed until a big play occurs. Then he watches closely and is aware of just the right moment to move in and make the saving tackle or deflect the long pass.

Neither of us knows a lot about football. But when we heard this, we thought, "That's it." That is exactly what this chapter is about. As adults who love adolescents, we are the defensive backs in the deepest position. We love them from the background, watching for when we're needed, and then we kick into gear. That is precisely what moms like Deb have done. They have been safeties in the deepest position or the home plate their adolescents can return to when they have faced danger. And they have invited their children to the safe place they have discovered...the Hope that holds them fast.

5
Stargazing

There are some things that should be as they are:
Plain, unadorned, common and all-complete;
Unmuddled and unmeddled with;
The straight, the smooth, the salt, the sour, the sweet.
For all that's timeless, untutored, untailored and untooled;
For innocence unschooled;
For unploughed prairies, primal snow and sod,
Water unmuddied, wind unruled,
For these, thank God.

Singly and strongly, from each separate star
a brightness pricks the retina from far
to near. And for clear eyes to see deep space and dark infinity
with an untroubled gaze, give praise.[1]

—LUCI SHAW, *A SONG FOR SIMPLICITY*

"I know exactly what my favorite time was."

It was the last day of ninth- and tenth-grade Summer Sessions. We were reflecting back over the week, each camper sharing with the group what had been the most memorable experience for him. In a roomful of adolescents, we expected there would be lots of voices saying things like, "learning to water-ski," "riding the banana boat backwards," and "knocking John off the tube." Instead, what we heard over and over was what one 14-year-old said, "My favorite time was the night Adam had the idea for all of the guys to go hang out on the top of the dock. Justin took his guitar, and we looked up at the stars and talked. I even saw my first falling star. It was awesome!"

Despite all the fun of inner tubes, ski boats, and rope swings, almost every boy at camp talked about how meaningful they found the night on the dock. There was nothing to entertain them that evening. No planning took place beforehand. There were no skits, no video games, and not even any girls. It was just a group of teenage boys sitting on the dock, looking at the stars.

The Allure of Simplicity

Simplicity. Just the mention of the word probably brings to mind images of hammocks, summer evening walks, the first snowfall, and stargazing. Simplicity. It is something each of us longs for, but which few experience with any kind of regularity. So, we watch reruns of Andy Griffith and remember what it was like (or dream about what it would be like) to live in Small Town, America.

We even go as far as to create our own versions of Small Town, America. This morning, we were having breakfast with a friend who talked about her time growing up in Monteagle, just a few hours from Nashville, where cottage after cozy cottage line the streets of the little community, which lies atop Monteagle Mountain. The description made Sissy think of Epworth Heights located on Lake Michigan, where her grandparents spend their summers. In both of these beautiful spots, families not only vacation, but also live in simplicity for the summer. If you were to drive through either place, as our friend Pace did yesterday, you would see people working in their gardens. Families grill outdoors every night and adults go for walks, stopping to talk with their neighbors on front porches. In the middle of the afternoon, the kids disappear for their mandatory rest time. In the late afternoon, you see these same kids race on their bikes to the ice-cream shop.

Teenagers gather every night on the sand dunes to sit by the fire and talk.

We hear these descriptions and sigh. *We long for simplicity. We just can't remember how to find it in the midst of the chaos that overwhelms our lives.*

As Kim Thomas wrote, "It seems that the muchness, the manyness, and the busyness have caused us to trip over our lives, and we just hope to get to the end of the day in time to turn out the lights before the tenacious sun shows its face for another day."[2]

As adults, most of us are very aware of this longing for simplicity. You may be surprised, however, to hear that adolescents share the same desire. For them, chaos is taking place in their outer and inner lives and they are looking for a little peace and simplicity.

Here is the schedule of a typical adolescent: They awaken (at least 15 minutes after they are supposed to), get directly in the shower, have breakfast (if there's time), and leave for school. They race from class to class, gulp down a quick lunch, all the while having fleeting conversations with friends. After school they have any number of activities, such as cheerleading practice, soccer games, forensics, piano lessons, or part-time jobs. Afterwards, they go on to the next activity and then home for dinner. After finishing dinner, they do their homework, spend at least 30 minutes (though they would prefer two hours) on AOL or on the phone and then go to bed around 11 P.M.

A recent *Newsweek* article entitled "Stop Stressing Me" discusses the chaos of the outer lives of adolescents.

> While most kids today enjoy their endless whirl of lessons, games and practices, a growing number are finding that the hyperscheduled life of the modern American student is more than they can handle. The activities meant to enrich

> their lives can leave them feeling burned out—or
> dangerously overloaded. As Andrea, a junior in
> high school, told the *Newsweek* reporter: "I like
> being busy, but it got to a point where it was just
> way too much."[3]

As this article points out, many adolescents are experiencing burnout as a result of the vast number of activities taking place in their lives. To sit on a dock and talk is not only alluring because of the beauty of the stars, but primarily because it is a much-needed chance for these teenagers to slow down.

It is as difficult for adolescents to slow down their minds as it is for them to slow down their schedules. Their eyes have been opened to new realities on every level and they are suddenly hyperaware of what others think of them. They feel confusion over who they are and who they want to be. They are afraid of disappointing peers and parents. And new emotional and spiritual hungers are awakening in them at every turn.

During the same ninth- and tenth-grade camp as the stargazing gathering, we had an evening by the bonfire when many kids made decisions to commit or recommit their lives to Christ. We alternated between singing and giving the kids an opportunity to share. After one of the songs ended, a 15-year-old girl exclaimed, "I have never felt anything like this in my life! It's amazing. I feel like for the first time I really know God loves me and forgives me!" A few others shared similar feelings, and then we sang a few more songs. Then another 15-year-old girl said, "I hate to admit this to you all. I just don't feel anything. Everyone is saying all these wonderful, touchy-feely things about God, and I just don't feel any of them. I don't know what's wrong with me." Immediately, the first girl to speak lowered her head and quietly said, "Me, too. I felt great for a little while, but now I don't feel anything. I was so close to God, and now it's just gone. I wish somebody could help me."

What a picture of the tumultuousness going on inside the heads of adolescents. In any given 30-minute period, they can (and often do) run the gamut from elation to sadness, hope to despair, joy to misery. The chaos of their schedules is matched, and many times overshadowed, by the chaos of thoughts and feelings going on inside them.

Year after year, the teenagers that walk into Melissa's lakehouse for camp say, "I have missed it here so much." What they have missed the most is the simplicity. At camp, they are removed from the "muchness, manyness, and busyness" of their lives. They are in a safe place where they are free to enjoy relationships. They play hours of chess and checkers and are overjoyed to sit on a dock and look at the stars.

So, that's camp, you may be saying. How in the world can I have that kind of environment in my home? It is possible, we believe, to at least capture moments of this kind of simplicity. First, we must examine the obstacles that stand in the way of simplicity. Then, as we examine the life of Christ, we will see our way through to finding the simplicity that He modeled for us.

The Obstacles to Simplicity

On any given night in countless cities across the country, teenagers are doing the same thing: cruising. We both did it, Melissa around the Dairy Queen in Murray, Kentucky, and Sissy through Reservoir Park in Little Rock, Arkansas. Teenagers pile into the car of whoever has turned 16 first, and drive. They drive to find their friends. They drive to find whichever member of the opposite sex is holding their attention at the present time. They drive to connect with each other.

The movie theater nearest our office is where the teenagers hang out who are not yet old enough to cruise. Their parents drop them off to see a movie, and they spend more time standing outside the theater talking than they do actually watching the movie. This is because adolescents long for the simplicity of relationship and, when left to their own, build their activities around these relationships.

Unfortunately for adolescents, we are the ones who sometimes hinder the simplicity they long for. Between the muchness, manyness, and busyness of our endeavors to help them navigate life, we sometimes create the obstacles.

Muchness

"I'm bored" is something we frequently hear from the mouths of adolescents. In today's microwave society, children grow up overstimulated and overentertained. Because they are used to this, they come to expect it. This cultural phenomenon, when added to the brooding adolescent veneer, can keep us jumping through hoops to keep them engaged. We begin to act more like cruise directors than parents or youth leaders.

We take them on retreats and fill their time with speakers, games, and activities to hold their interest. On family vacations, we fill every moment with something that we hope will guarantee their enjoyment, like giant swings in Florida or amusement parks in Dallas. We are always seeking their positive response, which we know we'll never fully gain—simply because they are adolescents.

We need to slow down and move toward simplicity. We need to realize that we are chasing the proverbial carrot on a stick. We'll never receive the feedback we really want from our adolescents and we are usually causing more harm than good by continuing to seek it. We're furthering appetites in them that we know from our own experience can never be filled.

About a month ago, the kids who interned with us for the summer headed back to college. One girl was leaving home for the first time. On her way to school, she and her dad took a detour to climb Mount Leconte in Gatlinburg, Tennessee. Mount Leconte is a steep, challenging mountain with a rustic lodge located on top. The only way to get to or from the scenic lodge is to spend several hours hiking. Once there, you are free to rest and enjoy good food and conversation, without all the amenities of things like electricity.

This is simplicity. This father and daughter took the time to slow down and enjoy each other before she went away to school. It would have been easy for them to take a detour to a big city to shop and stay in a nice hotel. And there wouldn't have been anything wrong in doing so. But they had much more time for conversation on the mountain than they would ever have had in a mall. For the daughter, the trip was like a rest stop before a difficult journey. She walked away feeling loved and valued instead of simply entertained.

Manyness

As Gail Godwin wrote, "Young people aren't being given the necessary minimum of intangibles to grow on. They suffer from psychic undernourishment. Wisdom is developed in young human brains by the curriculum of conversation, thought, imagination, empathy, and reflection. Young people need to generate language and ideas, not just listen and watch as passive consumers."[4]

It is astounding how few families eat together anymore. We have, for the most part, lost the art of conversation. Between working late, games and practices, Bible studies, and many other good things, we simply can't coordinate our schedules to work in a family dinner.

We live most of our lives on the run. It seems like the best time to talk to our kids is in the car on the way to the next activity. But between the muchness of entertainment and the manyness of our chaotic lives, there is little space or time in which we can live. One of the reasons adolescents love spending time in their rooms is that they have time and space to simply be. They are free to imagine, have conversations, think, and reflect. (They are also free to listen to music at whatever volume they prefer!)

We need to slow down and move toward simplicity. It is important that our homes be different from the outside, chaotic world. Even though they will not say it, adolescents long for the same simplicity we do. We all need family dinners together.

One of the times kids love at camp is mealtime. Maybe it's because we do our meals a little differently than other camps. We don't have cooks, we have campers. Before each camp, we assign kids to a meal schedule. Over the course of a week, each child will help prepare about three meals. Believe it or not, they love this time. They enjoy the conversations that take place while grilling chicken or chopping tomatoes, and they feel a confidence that comes from creating and offering the group a delicious meal. They also enjoy sitting and partaking of the meals they have created. The second- to fourth-grade campers finish a meal in less than 20 minutes. The high school kids, however, usually linger at the table for over an hour. They love to talk.

It's simple. Adolescents need intangibles. They need conversation, connection, time to reflect, and space to grow and discover. And we need to create homes and places where this can occur.

Encourage your adolescent to keep a journal. Give them their own place in the yard to create a garden. Allow them time to spend in their rooms, music or no music. Help them discover the pleasure of a good book. Eat together.

Cook together. Enjoy each other in the simplicity that comes with relationship.

Busyness

If we were to think of a city that symbolizes busyness, we would think of New York City. We are writing this on September 30, 2001, 19 days after the tragedy of the World Trade Center, having just returned, along with our friend and coworker David, from helping with the relief efforts in New York. It is a different city than it used to be. People have slowed down considerably. They look each other in the eyes, and the hunger for spiritual and emotional connection is palpable. What we saw is a great picture of how our loving and gracious God redeems tragedy. He is using this time to draw folks to Him for safety. He is making known, through countless individuals, the hope that is found in Him alone.

One afternoon we were walking beside Central Park when we met a couple pushing a stroller with a dog alongside. We talked to them about the difference in New York since the terrorist attacks, commenting on the kindness of everyone we had met since we arrived. "People in New York have always been kind," the young woman said. "We've just been in too much of a hurry to show it."

These words are powerful, spoken by a woman who had recently endured tremendous grief. She had slowed down, recognizing the futility of busyness as well as her need for connection and simplicity.

Sometimes we practice this same futility with our adolescents. We become too busy for simple kindness. And as a result, they do not learn the value that can be found therein. Few things free us to be who we are like kindness. When people are kind, we feel safer. We feel encouraged and enjoyed.

One of the boys at Daystar drew a caricature of the significance we place on kindness at Daystar. In his cartoon, a group of boys are sitting in David's office. In front of David's chair is a button, and over his door is a gigantic paddle. David is reaching over to touch the button when he says, in the bubble above his head, "I told you guys what would happen if you didn't say hello to Melissa and call her by name when she walked in the room."

Obviously, we don't paddle the kids in our group counseling sessions. What we will do, though, is walk in a door and greet all the kids by name. If they don't say hello back, we'll walk out the door and knock, and try again. We will continue this until all of them look up, say hello, and speak our names. As you can imagine, sometimes this takes several tries with adolescents.

We need to slow down and move toward simplicity. Kindness is a significant part of that simplicity. When we are kind, our kids see the value in other people.

We cannot, however, settle for only being a model of kindness. Sometimes we will have to ensure that our children are communicating kindness to others. We may even have to walk in the door 17 times, but it is of the utmost importance that they learn to value each other, especially in the face of the terrible realities of our time.

The Simplicity of Christ

The ultimate example of simplicity is found in the life of Christ. He lived in kindness, careful not to become entangled in the webs of muchness, manyness, and busyness.

Many of Jesus' teachings begin with phrases like, "as he was going out," "and on the way," "as he came down the mountain," "and sitting down," and "while he was reclining at the table." Jesus chose to teach His disciples wherever He happened to be at the moment. Few places in Scripture contain verses in which Jesus sends His disciples out to gather the multitudes so that He can teach. Jesus didn't hold many seminars. He didn't use the ancient equivalents of overheads and workbooks. Instead, He spent the majority of His time walking, eating, and talking with a few folks who gave up their lives to follow Him.

Jesus' example leads us to see the sacrament in simplicity. He shared countless meals with His disciples. After His resurrection, Jesus spent his last few moments on earth sharing one such meal with His disciples.

> Jesus said to them, "Come and have breakfast." None of the disciples dared ask him, "Who are you?" They knew it was the Lord. Jesus came, took the bread and gave it to them, and did the same with the fish (John 21:12-13).

Each Sunday in many churches, people share a meal commemorating Jesus' life given for us. It is a sacrament of the Christian church, and it is called communion. We share this sacrament because on the night Jesus was betrayed, He commanded us to.

> And he took bread, gave thanks and broke it, and gave it to them, saying, "This is my body given for you; do this in remembrance of me." In the same way, after the supper he took the cup, saying, "This cup is the new covenant in my blood, which is poured out for you" (Luke 22:19-20).

Jesus speaks to us out of simplicity. He uses the everyday objects of bread and wine to reveal and signify His ultimate sacrifice for us. He shows us the way to the kind of simplicity that Madeleine L'Engle and Luci Shaw have written about:

Around the table we sit, as the candles flicker and burn down. We share ideas. We share food. We share our sense of calling, affirming again that we are here to do God's will and praying we will be given the grace to discern what God's will is. Love. Inclusion. Compassion. Openness. Willingness to listen to new ideas, to change. Lamb and potatoes. Bread and wine. Enjoyed together, in the understanding that all of life is a sacrament. We are companions.[5]

Simplicity cuts off useless reflections. It encourages thought, compassion, imagination, and conversation. It reminds us of the importance of kindness. Not only do we need to let go of the muchness, manyness, and busyness for our children, but also for ourselves. Jesus has commanded it. He calls us to slow down and to move toward simplicity. He calls us to live as He lived...to walk, talk, and eat with those we love. He calls us to see the sacrament in simplicity. It wouldn't be too difficult to picture Jesus Himself, lying in a field with His disciples, looking up at the stars, and talking.

6

Love and Laughter

Love and laughter abide in the holy family, which is the safest and sanest place for laughter. There it is free and fearless. When there are problems, love, like a surgeon, can cleanse and heal and remove suffering; and laughter, in love's hands, can be its scalpel or its healing balm. Laughter in love's hands is never used amiss, never mocks, never hurts. Just as human beings are at their best when they love, so, too, laughter is at its best when it arises out of love. Love and laughter ripen and bloom together in the Day of the Lord, or on any holy day.[1]

—G.K. CHESTERTON, *ALL THINGS CONSIDERED*

"Love and laughter abide in the holy family." The question is, do they abide in our families? Love most certainly does. For many families with adolescents, however, laughter is often in short supply. *One of the most difficult tasks of parenting adolescents can be simply enjoying them.*

- "How am I supposed to enjoy my son when he won't come out of his room?"

- "The only thing my daughter enjoys is her friends. I don't know how to enjoy her when she won't stay off the computer long enough to even have a conversation with me."

- "All my daughter wants to do with me is spend my money. I sure don't enjoy that!"

- "I can't enjoy someone who is angry with me all of the time."

These are all very natural responses for parents of adolescents. It is incredibly difficult, at times, to enjoy teenagers. They are usually entrenched in themselves and can be self-absorbed, unresponsive, sullen, and demanding...all at the same time.

In contrast, it is simple to enjoy young children. We take great delight in almost everything our babies do...from smiling to cooing to sleeping. We enjoy watching our toddlers learn and explore. We take great pleasure in helping our elementary school children begin to read. We enjoy our middle school children in their hunger to spend time with us. And then it hits. Seemingly overnight the shift to teenagedom occurs, and we are left scrambling to do what used to seem so natural. So how do we enjoy our adolescents?

In this chapter, we'll talk about the necessity for love and laughter in our homes because love is the active part of enjoyment. Love gives us the ability to enjoy our adolescents even when they are difficult to enjoy.

Love

It is easy for us to love that which is lovable, and it is easy to enjoy that which is enjoyable...good food, interesting books, and people who are kind. For many of the things we enjoy, we are passive as consumers.

But with adolescents, neither love nor enjoyment can be passive. For us to take pleasure in them has more to do with us than it does with them. It may be very difficult to find things that we relish in them. We may have trouble finding things in common that we like. Often it will not be easy to enjoy them, not because of who they are but because of where they are developmentally.

We once overheard a group of adolescent girls having the following conversation about their parents.

"I hate it when my mom sings in the car. It's so embarrassing."

"I hate it when I have a friend over to spend the night and my dad walks outside to get the paper in his *bath robe!* It's humiliating."

"I can't believe my mom thinks I would want to go to the mall and walk around with her and my little sisters. There is no way I would do that."

One of the main reasons it is difficult to enjoy adolescents is that they don't seem to enjoy us. They no longer have the need they once had for our time and attention. They're embarrassed to spend time with us in public. They definitely don't want us to try to teach them anything or share with them something we might be learning. And they are humiliated when we feel free to be ourselves in front of their friends.

So, what do we do? How do we enjoy them when they seem developmentally unenjoyable and no longer able to enjoy us? This becomes one of the primary tasks of those who love adolescents: to be free to enjoy them whether they respond or not. And isn't this the very definition of love?

> *You have heard that it was said, "Love your neighbor and hate your enemy." But I tell you: Love your enemies and pray for those who persecute you, that you may be sons of your Father in heaven....If you love those who love you, what reward will you get? Are not even the tax collectors doing that? And if you greet only your brothers, what are you doing more than others? Do not even pagans do that?*
>
> —MATTHEW 5:43-45A; 46-47

Hopefully, it has not reached the point where we would consider our adolescents to be our enemy. But biblical love *is* about caring for those who are difficult to love. It is active, not passive. It pursues. For those of us in relationship with adolescents, this is our challenge. Whether they are enjoying us or not, we still need to enjoy them. Our ability to do so has a great deal to do with where our own sense of enjoyment comes from.

The Origins of Our Enjoyment

Our Faith

Bob Benson wrote in *See You at the House:*

> I asked Patrick if he could describe what it was like marching toward the stands filled with cheering parents and friends, playing wide open with all that paint on his face and finally coming to attention as the last echoes of the music of the concluding song of the final show are lost in the noise of the crowd. He grinned as if it were impossible to explain. I told him that if he thought it was exciting on the field he should just wait until a day somewhere, sometime when he was a dad at a state championship. And then he would see his kid turn and march toward him in perfect step with a hundred other kids, his head high and his back straight, beating fifty pounds of drums as if it were his task to set the tempo for the whole world. I told him if I was still around, I wanted to be sitting there with him. And then we can talk about what thrilling really is.
>
> My thinking about this nudged me into some further thoughts about the heavenly Father. This one who is calling us. We all tend to believe (or at least fear) that the God who calls us is

watching us. It makes all the difference in the world where we think he is sitting. As long as we think of him as the judge in the pressbox who is checking for smudges on our white shoes, for the misplayed notes, for marching out of step, for our hats falling off, or any one of a dozen other things that can happen to us in a performance, it is hard to keep from living our whole lives in fear of a button coming off our tunics.

It was Jesus himself who reminded us that we were to call him Father—"Abba Father"—which is a lot more like calling him Dad. I think Jesus was telling us that our Father is the one in the stands who is standing on the seat, waving his coat in a circle over his head, with tears of pride and happiness running down his face.[2]

As God's children, we are loved and enjoyed immensely. 1 John 4:19 says, "We love because he first loved us." It could also be said, We enjoy because he first enjoyed us. Our faith is our springboard. Colossians 3:12 refers to us as "God's chosen people, holy and dearly loved." We learn to love our children dearly as we come to understand that we are dearly loved.

The Westminster Catechism states, "The chief end of man is to glorify God and enjoy Him forever." As we glorify and enjoy God, our hearts are changed. When we are in relationship with Christ, He is continually transforming us into His image. We learn to love and enjoy as He loves and enjoys. And as we are transformed, so is our parenting. Therefore, when we are living our lives in response to God's love for us, our adolescents will reap the benefits.

Our Memory

In his book, *A Long Obedience in the Same Direction*, Eugene Peterson dedicates an entire chapter to joy, using

Psalm 126 to illustrate that both our memory and our hope are the origins of that joy. As Peterson wrote:

> The center sentence in the psalm is 'We are one happy people' (v. 3). The words on one side of that center (vv. 1-2) are in the past tense, the words on the other side (vv. 4-6) in the future tense. Present gladness has past and future.[3]

The first two verses of the Psalm outline the great things God has done for His people which contribute to their happiness. Similarly, He has done great things for us. When our adolescents are at their least enjoyable, we can always remember the blessings of our past with them. Many parents who bring their adolescents in for counseling will say something like, "I still remember when he was such a sweet little boy."

We don't even have to reach as far back as their childhood though, to find moments of enjoyment. If we look closely, God will give us glimpses of the children we love even through the haze of their adolescence.

- "There is something about the time right before he goes to bed. He will still let me sit down on his bed and pray with him. He actually talks to me."

- "In the car is when we have our best talks. On the way to soccer practice last night, she broke down and finally told me what was wrong."

Our memory of the past has immense power for our enjoyment of the present. In their book *Cry of the Soul*, Dan Allender and Tremper Longman speak of the importance of our memory: "To remember the past is to reshape the present with desire and hope."[4]

Desire and hope can be the by-products of memory. It is important that we remember and cherish the times of enjoyment with our children, both recent and in times past. As we bring to mind these moments, we are given a glimpse of who they really are—more than just a frustrating teen. That makes us better able to love and enjoy them in the present and gives us the desire and hope we need to press on through this tumultuous time.

Our Hope

Hope is crucial to enjoying our adolescents. The second section of Psalm 126 (vv. 4-6) talks about the future. This is where hope comes in. Not only do God's people remember the great things He has done for them, but they look forward to seeing Him fulfill His promises to them in the future. They have hope. We can have the same type of hope for our adolescents.

Each month we have a moms' breakfast for the mothers of the kids who are in counseling at Daystar. The purpose of this group is for these moms to share hope with each other. We begin the time by taking turns, with each mom sharing about her child and the reasons she brought him or her in for counseling. Every time these stories are shared, so is hope. The moms of the older adolescents say to the moms of the younger ones, "You won't know exactly when it happens. One day, you'll wake up and he'll have turned a corner. He will notice something that you've done for him or introduce you to his friends, and you'll realize he's back. He's an older version of the boy you once knew, but he's definitely back."

These moms all had to walk through the struggles of adolescence with their children. What they are trying to share with the moms of younger adolescents is hope. They know the frustration of loving adolescents who are unresponsive. They know what it's like to have all of their attempts at enjoyment met with embarrassment. But they also know the power of hope. They know and trust God's promise that He is working in their children. They have faith in Him and in who He is creating their children to be. They echo Paul's words:

> *I thank my God every time I remember you. In all my prayers for all of you, I always pray with joy because of your partnership in the gospel from the first day until now, being confident of this, that he who began a good work in you will carry it on to completion until the day of Christ Jesus.*
>
> —PHILIPPIANS 1:3-6

God has begun a good work in every one of us, including our adolescents. In this verse, Paul goes back to the past and looks toward the present with gratitude. In his faith, he prays with joy. Our enjoyment can come from the same places.

God has done great things for us, just as He did for the people in Psalm 126. He graciously loves and enjoys us. He has given us hearts that can love and adolescents to share that love with. He is completing a good work in them, and in us. As we lean on our faith in Him, the memories of our past, and our hope for the future of our adolescents, we are freed to love and enjoy them.

Laughter

We have a friend who laughs all the time. Spending time with Juliana makes both of us feel like we're really funny, even though that's not necessarily true. Her laughter is contagious. The longer we are with her, the lighter we feel.

Reinhold Niebuhr once said, "What is funny about us is precisely that we take ourselves too seriously." As parents and those who love adolescents, it is easy for us to take ourselves too seriously. We can get caught up in the adolescent drama, and instead of feeling lighter, our hearts become weighted down with frustration. That's why we not only need love in our homes but laughter as well.

There are, of course, different kinds of laughter. One type of laughter is what we might call artificial laughter. Into this category we list sarcasm, laughter at the expense of someone else, or laughter over inappropriate things. These are probably the most common forms of teenage laugher. Teens make fun of each other constantly and have a tendency to be flippant, cruel, and cynical. Bodily noises and humor about bodily functions seem to be the height of humor for them, and sarcasm tends to be their predominant vernacular.

One of the rules for our counseling groups and camps is that sarcasm is not allowed. This rule is part of our attempt to create a safe place. When groups started up last September, we were going over the group rules with the kids. One of the high school girls said, "No sarcasm is definitely the hardest rule for me. It's how my family relates to each other and I relate to my friends. I don't know any other way to be funny."

But there is another type of laughter that is healing, the kind Chesterton speaks of in the quote at the beginning of this chapter. It is what we would call genuine laughter. It is laughter that makes us feel lighter and frees us to be ourselves by making us forget about ourselves.

Martin Luther saw the importance of this kind of laughter. As he once wrote, "It is pleasing to the dear God whenever thou rejoicest or laughest from the bottom of thy heart." Where artificial laughter tends to exclude others, genuine laughter invites others to join in. It creates an atmosphere of enjoyment.

One of our summer camp traditions has become "Christmas in July." We take the kids to the small town of Hazel, Kentucky, where they each have $3 to spend on a gift. The gifts are supposed to be symbolic of what the recipient means to the giver. This past summer, a ninth-grade girl drew Melissa's name. The anticipation built as she talked about how Melissa is like a covering over us, protecting and shielding us. She handed Melissa her gift, which happened to be an authentic grass skirt. Melissa promptly put on the skirt and did a hula dance in front of the entire camp. Needless to say, Melissa was in stitches. She laughed and laughed until tears were streaming down her face. Her genuine laughter invited us all to share in the enjoyment. By the end of her hula performance, every person in the room had joined in the laughter.

As parents, don't we want to create this kind of atmosphere of enjoyment with our adolescents (minus the hula skirts)? We want to invite them to experience genuine laughter and to feel lighter. And we want them to be freed to be themselves by forgetting about themselves. We want to learn what it means to enjoy them, regardless of their response.

This kind of atmosphere is created not only by actual laughter, but also by curiosity, spontaneity, and commonality.

Curiosity

One of the greatest gifts we can give someone we care for is our curiosity. We feel honored when someone takes the time and really asks us how we are. Melissa has two aunts, Aunt Robbie and Aunt Emmy Lou, who offered her the gift of curiosity during her growing-up years. When she went to Aunt Robbie's house, her aunt made fried chicken and homemade rolls and asked Melissa all kinds of questions about her life. They spent hours laughing, eating, and telling stories. When her Aunt Emmy Lou flew in from California, Melissa and her two brothers each vied to get their own personal time with her. She always wanted to talk about all that was going on in their lives and was interested in hearing every detail. A wonderful little book called *Mrs. Miniver* that was written during World War II talks about the importance of aunts for this very purpose. In the book, Aunt Hetty speaks to Mrs. Miniver of her frustration over the children all growing up.

> "From an aunt's point of view it's unpardonable. Between the lot of you, you ought to have arranged things better. What on earth d'you think I'm here for, I should like to know?"
>
> To be a pattern and example to all aunts, thought Mrs. Miniver; to be a delight to boys and a comfort to their parents; and to show that at least one daughter in every generation ought to remain unmarried, raise the profession of auntship to a fine art, and make a point of having a house within the five-mile limit, preferable between Boveney and Queen's Eyeot.[5]

The same could be said of uncles, grandparents, teachers, youth directors, and adult friends. Adolescents love to talk about themselves. They expect their parents to ask questions, but are surprised and delighted when someone else is curious about them. One of the predominant ways we can enjoy them is through our curiosity.

Where does this leave parents? Adolescents tend to feel interrogated when asked questions by their parents. Remember that curiosity is very different from interrogation. As we know, adolescents hate to be asked questions like "How was your day?" "How did you do on your test?" and "How was youth group?" They meet each of these questions with a snarl or a grunt. We tend to ask our children the questions we want to be asked, but these are usually not the questions they want to answer. They hate to feel like we are prying. We have known parents who, when their children don't want to talk, follow them into their rooms until the adolescents answer their questions. This is not curiosity. It is interrogation.

Enjoy them. Ask them questions; be curious. But give them a choice. Don't force them to talk. This will only silence them further. Be creative in your questions. Whereas they tend to slam the door when we ask about school, they may ramble at length when we ask about their friends. Later in the chapter, we'll talk about the importance of finding places to connect with our children. Ask questions about these places. Pull in family members and friends who love your children and can be curious, as well. As Hillary Rodham Clinton quoted from an old African proverb, "It takes a village to raise a child." It sometimes can take a village just to enjoy our adolescents.

Spontaneity

Melissa will never forget an instance one Christmas when her family experienced spontaneous enjoyment. Her mom asked each family member to fill a water glass to a different level and then instructed them to play Christmas carols by hitting the glasses with spoons. Everyone groaned about it in the beginning but ended up having a ball.

Several years ago, we experienced a societal shift toward the concept of "quality time." It is important to have quality time with our families...time we have set aside to invest in them. It is also important, however, to have spontaneous time. In the midst of the craziness of adolescents' schedules, we may only have a chance for "quality time" once a week. We have opportunities for spontaneous time every day.

The mother of an eighth grader recently talked about the chaos of her daughter's schedule. "I actually really love it," she said. "We spend so much time in the car when it's just us that we get to talk a lot. When she's away from the distractions of her brothers, her friends, and the phone, she'll talk to me."

This is a good example of making the most of spontaneous time. When Sissy was in high school, her mom used to stay up every night until she got home. Sissy always thought it was to make sure she came in at curfew. Years later when they talked about it, her mom said, "Oh, no. I stayed up because that was the time you talked the most."

We need to look for spontaneous opportunities. Quality time is a great thing, but it is also important that we enjoy our adolescents in the midst of everyday life. Sometimes we are so caught up in planning our quality times that we miss these moments when they appear.

At summer camps, our boats break down constantly. We have decided that God does this on purpose. Every time a boat breaks down, a great conversation comes out of it. The kids come together as a group to help fix the boat.

Adolescents are spontaneous creatures. They constantly fly by the seat of their pants. Part of learning to enjoy them has to do with connecting with them where they are. If your daughter is talking to you in the car, don't drive straight home, take advantage of the moment. Pull over and get ice cream. Take the long route home. If we have the courage to let go of our own agendas, we can learn to go with the spontaneity of the moment. As a result, we can enjoy our adolescents in ways we never could have planned.

Commonality

We talked before about the importance of finding places to connect with our adolescents. This can be difficult. We probably don't have a great deal in common with them. Most likely we're not particularly fond of their taste in music, movies, or reading materials. We can't connect with them in the same ways we would with adults.

But we still need to connect. As with spontaneity, finding things in common requires some creativity. For example, Sissy's grandparents loved to dance. On many afternoons when her dad, aunt, and uncle were growing up, they would invite their friends over to their house, push back the furniture in the living room, turn on the Four Tops, and dance. The kids, their friends, and their parents would dance together. Sissy's grandparents found that they had a love for dancing in common with their kids. They used that love as a place to connect with and enjoy their adolescents. Sissy's dad, aunt, and uncle have continued the same tradition with their own children. During Sissy's teenage years, one of her favorite memories was learning the jitterbug in the den with her dad. Across Little Rock and just next door, her cousins were dancing in their dens with their parents as well.

Enjoying adolescents can take place in a variety of settings. It can happen in a living room, at a football game, or on a walk. The connection can be over a shared activity or a shared relationship.

One mom we know struggled with her adolescent son for years. She tried and tried to connect with him only to have most of her attempts thwarted. After he went off to college, he bought a dog. When he came home to visit, he brought the dog with him. He recently moved home, along with his dog. Now, his mom has become as attached to the dog as he is. When these two have nothing else to talk about, they can talk about Muffin. Their shared love for the dog brings them together and helps them enjoy each other.

Curiosity, spontaneity, and commonality. Our faith, our memory, and our hope. Love and laughter. How do we enjoy that which can sometimes seem unenjoyable? We can start by leaning on these principles. We love our adolescents, and we laugh with them. We ask questions. We make the most of the moments given to us. We find places to connect. We draw on our past and our future to remember who God has created our teenagers to be. And we remember how enjoyed and dearly loved we are as God's children. He is the true source of all of our enjoyment.

> *There is nothing better for a man than to eat and drink and tell himself that his labor is good. This also I have seen that it is from the hand of God. For who can eat and who can have enjoyment without Him?*
>
> —ECCLESIASTES 2:24-25 NASB

Part Three

Shape

Shape

A piece of clay must be softened before it can take on any type of shape. We've learned that adolescents are a great deal like clay. By the time many children become teenagers, they have developed a hard exterior. The exterior may take the form of anger or it may be a resigned shrug of the shoulders that says, "I don't care." It may even be a smile that serves more as a smoke screen than an expression of happiness.

Once we walk in the back door of our adolescent's heart, we may be surprised to bump into this hard exterior. Whichever form it takes, it serves the same purpose. It stops us. It prevents us from going any further with our adolescents. It hinders us from being who we are called to be in their lives: those who help them see and become who God has created each of them to be.

In Part Two, we examined what softening looks like in the lives of our adolescents. Softening breaks down the hard exterior. It helps us move past the anger, the shrug of the shoulders, and the phony smile so that we can truly connect with our adolescents.

Softening occurs within the context of relationship. The relationship that we offer our adolescents can be one that reflects safety, simplicity, and enjoyment. As we become safe places for our adolescents, we can invite them to know true safety in Christ. Following His model of simplicity, we can provide them a haven from the muchness, manyness, and busyness that encompasses their lives. And finally, as we let go of our own agendas and allow ourselves to truly enjoy our teenagers, we also are transformed by the love and laughter that fill our homes.

Softening always takes place before shaping.

As the hearts of adolescents are softened, then shaping can begin. Whereas softening involves safety, simplicity, and enjoyment, shaping involves the principles of imagination, respect, and gratitude. The next three chapters will be devoted to each of these principles.

Thankfully, it is God who ultimately shapes adolescents. "Yet, O Lord, you are our Father. We are the clay, you are the potter; we are all the work of your hand" (Isaiah 64:8). He does, however, use us in the process. As adults who love adolescents, we, in essence, are the potter's assistants. He works through our imagination, respect, and gratitude to shape our children. We join Him at the potter's wheel in shaping our teenagers into whom He has created each of them to be.

7

A Great Big Bundle of Potentiality

I am a promise. I am a possibility.
I am a promise, with a capital P.
I am a great big bundle of potentiality.
And I am learning to hear God's voice,
and I am trying to make the right choice.
I am a promise to be anything God wants me to be.[1]

—BILL AND GLORIA GAITHER

Melissa and her nephew, George, used to sit under the dining room table to talk. They would get under the table to escape all the noise and confusion that often accompanies family gatherings. There they would talk, laugh, and sing. The song they sang would always be the same: "I Am a Promise" by Bill and Gloria Gaither. They would sing this song not only because George loved it but also because it was a reflection of who God was creating George to be.

Maybe we need to get under the table and sing with our adolescents. But because they probably would be humiliated to get under the table and sing with us, maybe our getting under the table with adolescents is figurative rather than literal.

God has placed us specifically in the lives of each adolescent we care about for a purpose. Part of our purpose is to remind them of theirs.

Melissa used to meet with a group of middle school boys that included a sixth grader named Tom. Tom was the one in the group who talked the loudest, laughed the most, and tried the hardest to get everyone's attention. He was constantly being pulled out of the group. One afternoon he was extremely angry and acted very rude to the other boys. As was customary, Melissa pulled Tom out of the group to talk to him. When they walked into the hall, Melissa put her hand on Tom's shoulder and said, "Tom, I want you to listen to me."

"I know what you're going to say," Tom shouted in reply. "You're going to say I've got PO-TENTIAL!"

Tom was exactly right. Melissa was going to remind him of his potential, and his purpose. She wanted Tom to know that he mattered, to her and to the group.

This is a crucial part of the shaping that takes place in the lives of adolescents. In the last section of the book, we talked about the importance of relationship. Shaping cannot take place without it. Adolescents will slam the door in our faces every time if we try to shape them outside of the context of relationship.

What do we mean by shaping? As we stated in the introduction, shaping means the actual movement of the adolescent. It means helping them become the person who God has created each of them to be. Shaping teenagers is often the part we feel most comfortable with as adults. A lot of the time we spend with adolescents is time devoted to teaching. What we want this chapter to do, however, is to challenge the ways we traditionally think of shaping. We want to step out of the classroom and into the lives of our adolescents by understanding their worlds. We want to shape more with imagination than by instruction. We want to get our hands dirty with humility as we develop a vision of who God is forming them to be. In this chapter, we will examine understanding, imagination, and humility and the power each has in our ability to connect with adolescents.

Understanding

For Sissy's thirtieth birthday, we went to her favorite place in America, Walt Disney World. Melissa had not been there since Epcot was built, so we devoted a day to each park. As we walked through the parks, there was one thing we were always trying to find: a map. Between all the lands at the Magic Kingdom, the countries at Epcot, and the movie sets at MGM, it was easy to get lost. The creators of the parks must have realized this, because they had maps placed throughout the parks. When we came to a map, the first thing we looked for was a large arrow with the words "You are here" written above it. This was crucial to finding our next adventure. For us to find The Country Bear Jamboree, we needed to know how to get there from Space Mountain, where we happened to be standing at the time.

The same is true with teenagers. We know they have PO-TENTIAL. We see the people who God is creating them to be. Our job, then, is to move past the seeing and to help them *become* that person. As we said before, shaping is the actual movement of the adolescent. Understanding is the foundation of shaping. It is the "You Are Here" sign written above the heads of our adolescent children.

A freshman in college came home for a weekend and announced to her mother that she no longer believed in God. This mother has walked through heartache after heartache and believes strongly in the power and mercy of God. Her heart fell to the floor as she heard her daughter say these words. The mom's response, however, was different than you might expect. The first thing she said was, "Don't tell your grandmother."

What she went on to say, however, was a great picture of understanding. "You know, you can go as far as you can go, but you'll always belong to Jesus. My concern is you'll make it hard on yourself. But, really, the people that question end up stronger than those who never question at all."

The *Expository Dictionary of Bible Words* states that one of the Hebrew words for understanding is *sakal*. "The verb *sakal* suggests a process of reasoning through complex situations to a practical conclusion, enabling one to act wisely."[2]

This mom demonstrated *sakal*. To respond with *sakal* is to respond with wisdom, rather than impulsiveness. She could have reacted in panic and said something like, "I can't believe you. Why are you trying to hurt me all the time?" She could have called the professor of the course that was causing her daughter to question her faith. But she didn't. She responded in a way that reminded her daughter of Jesus' love for her and the potential consequences of turning her back on that love. In the end, she gave her daughter a picture of who God is creating her to be...a young woman whose faith is stronger for having doubted.

Often the most natural thing in the world for us to do in response to our adolescents is to react. In reaction, the focus changes from them to us. This lets them off the hook, in effect. The emphasis changes from what the child has said or done to what the parent is doing. They can dismiss us by saying, "My mom is so emotional," or "My dad just doesn't understand."

Teenagers are in the process of changing. Their emotions, bodies, and brains are in a period of chaos. We hear kids say often, "I hate to be sad or angry around my parents. They make a bigger deal about things than I do and get more sad or angry than me. Why would I talk to them?" Our reactions can sometimes shut them down, preventing them from having their own feelings. Teenagers are going through a time of profound change. These changes are a part of their becoming. We may feel hurt or angry at their actions, or even at how someone has treated them, but our response has the power to free or stifle them. One of the best things we can do during this time is to remain constant and objective. This is an important part of understanding teenagers.

In an article published by *Newsweek* called "Mind Expansion: Inside the Teenage Brain," scientists outlined the growth taking place in brains of teenagers.

> Around puberty, the brain blossoms with new brain cells and neural connections, something that was thought to happen only in the first 18 months of life. Then, between puberty and young adulthood the frontal lobes—responsible for such "executive" functions as self-control, judgment, emotional regulation, organization and planning—undergo wholesale renovation.[3]

Adolescence is a period of extreme transition. The brains, bodies, and emotions of teenagers are changing dramatically. Their worlds are changing as well. These dramatic changes can add a great deal of chaos both in our homes and in our relationships with adolescents. Familiarize yourself with what is happening internally and externally in the lives of teenagers. Read magazine articles and books. Ask questions. Our understanding serves only to strengthen our relationships.

Understanding is sometimes one of the most difficult things for us to do. It is difficult because it feels like we are not *doing* anything. Elizabeth Goudge wrote: "If you understand people you're of use to them whether you can do anything tangible for them or not. Understanding is a creative act in a dimension we do not see."[4]

In some ways, understanding is more for us than for our adolescents. It enables us to respond out of wisdom rather than panic. Understanding gives us the perspective to see who our adolescents are before we can have the imagination to help them become whom God has created them to be.

Imagination

Imagination is the capacity to see what might not yet appear but should.[5]
—CAROLINE J. SIMON

There is a scene in the movie *Hook* that we both love. In it, Peter Panning (Peter Pan grown up) has been challenged by Rufio (the current leader of the Lost Boys). Rufio draws a line in the sand, daring the boys to line up either beside him or beside Panning to declare their allegiance. All the boys except one move to the side of Rufio, who has both the skill and the sword. The one little boy who stays with Peter circles Peter several times. He makes Peter kneel down, removes Peter's glasses, and then uses his hands to massage Peter's face into a smile. He joyfully exclaims, "There you are, Peter," and the rest of the boys run to Peter's side.

This is imagination. This little boy saw what had not yet appeared but should be there in Peter Panning. He saw his PO-TENTIAL. Imagination builds on understanding by moving from who adolescents are to who they can be.

If there is anything that stays with the kids that attend our summer camps, it is the imagination. Each year at each camp, we have some type of theme. The theme has ranged from taking someone to the water (inspired by *The Lion King*) to giving new names (inspired by Revelation 2:17). The themes are different, but the outcome is the same. Before camp is over, each child sits in front of the group and is given a picture of who he can be. One by one, the campers speak to that child out of their imagination... offering a glimpse of who they believe God is creating that person to be.

One summer, Connie, a friend of ours, gave one such picture to Lauren. She had bought Lauren a gift that represented who Connie believed God was creating Lauren to be. As Lauren sat in front of the group, Connie unfolded a beautifully handcrafted tablecloth, which she spread before Lauren. She spoke at length about Lauren, about the way that she so freely offers her heart to others. "You spread out your life before us like a tablecloth, and invite others to join in the banquet. I see you living a life that not only invites others to know you, but also to deeply know Christ." As you can imagine, Lauren was profoundly touched. She still treasures the tablecloth and the memory of Connie's words.

Spreading tablecloths before our own children is hard to imagine. They would probably respond with an "Oh, mom," and go to their rooms and shut the door. We can, however, love them with an imagination that draws out their PO-TENTIAL.

We have two close friends, David and Sandy, who have been married for close to 35 years. They have three grown children whom we both love, as well. Over the years we have known David and Sandy, they have demonstrated this parental imagination. David and Sandy are imagination in action, but in entirely different ways.

David is engaging. He loves to talk and will sit down beside you and ask you question after question about your life. He responds with the utmost sincerity and concern. Before the end of the conversation, he will grab your hand and look you straight in the eye. His words will begin with "I see you..." and he will go on to tell you who he believes God is creating you to be. He lives out his imagination by spending time in conversation with people and calling out who they are becoming.

Sandy, on the other hand, rarely has time to sit down and talk. As she flies by preparing a meal, she squeezes your face and says, "I love YOU." She has a gift of rejoicing with others as she laughs from the bottom of her soul, and grieving with others as she sheds intense tears of pain with those who are hurting. Sandy's imagination is expressed in movement. To spend time with Sandy is to feel loved and enjoyed. That love and enjoyment, in itself, calls you to something bigger and greater than you are now.

For years, these two have had a constant flow of kids coming in and out of their home, including their own. Kids love to spend time there, knowing that they can openly share their struggles and failures. David will still say, "I see you..." and Sandy will still grab their faces and tell them she loves them.

How does this translate to our own children? How do we see past the behavior of our son—with imagination—when his sarcasm pushes everyone he loves away? How do we believe in and enjoy our daughter in a way that calls her to who God is creating her to be when the kids at school make fun of her because of her weight?

We pray. *We pray that God will give us a vision for who He is creating our children to be, and that He will give us the grace to love them out of that vision.* Even in counseling, it is easy to focus only on our client's behaviors, how we want them to change. With our children, it is the same. We see how they fail, how they are hurt, and how they hurt others. We want to understand this and then pray our way past it. God is the author of our salvation and our imagination. He can give us a vision for our children greater than any we would ever hope to have on our own. And He can give us the ability to live out that imagination in words and movement.

To believe in our children in this way is painful. We remember the words from Galatians 4:19: "...I am again in the pains of childbirth until Christ is formed in you...." It hurts us, at times, to see who they are now. When a daughter comes home drunk for the first time, when a son has stolen a stereo from the neighbor's car, when a daughter is the only one not invited to the prom, when a son with a learning disability is humiliated in front of his class...the list goes on and on. Every parent has tasted the pain of or for a child. To do so causes us tremendous grief. It is difficult to see past the hurt and into their hearts. But we can, with God's help.

> *I pray also that the eyes of your heart may be*
> *enlightened in order that you may know the hope*
> *to which he has called you....*
>
> —EPHESIANS 1:18A

Humility

Humility brings understanding and imagination together. With understanding, we enter the worlds of our adolescents. We see life from their perspective. Imagination enlarges that perspective and calls out what is deeper. With imagination, we help them become who God is creating them to be. Humility makes all of this possible.

To understand and have imagination without humility sets us up in a place of exaggerated authority in our adolescents' lives. We sit above them, puffing ourselves up with our understanding and imagination. This exaggerated authority is seen as a challenge by adolescents. They see it as an invitation to the struggle for power. It is like the childhood game where everyone stands in a circle and puts their hands on top of each other's. The pile of hands climbs higher and higher, as each player tries to keep his hand on the top. The stakes get too high (higher than the heads of the children playing), and the game has to stop. Power struggles operate similarly. The stakes get higher and higher as we go, and our children end up going so far to prove their own sense of power that they make foolish, sometimes dangerous, decisions.

To understand and have imagination with humility brings us close to our adolescents. With humility, we step out of the power struggle. We become their servants, rather than simply their superiors.

What does this mean for a youth director, a counselor, or a parent? As a youth director, it means moving to the background and letting the kids take the leadership. They can do this by leading worship, helping minister to other kids in their group, and assisting in planning their retreats. For counselors, it means coming out from behind a desk and putting down your notepad. Sit with teenagers, be interested in them, believe that they have something to say, and really respond to them. For parents, it means respecting them, which we will talk more about in the next chapter. Respect them by allowing them to make choices within the boundaries of what you feel is appropriate. They feel honored when we trust that they can make choices (even when we know in our hearts that they may and often will fail).

Several summers ago, we were trying to teach a high school boy to water-ski. The boat was full of kids. We got him in the water with his skis on and with all the slack out of the rope. We gunned the motor, there was a great splash behind the boat, and he fell. We circled around...made sure his skis were still on and all the slack was once again out of the line, and we gunned the motor. There was again a great splash, and he fell. This time when we circled around, the kids in the boat started shouting out to him, "Keep your skis together! Bend your knees! Keep your arms straight!" He grunted in answer, and we tried again. This happened over and over until the shouts from the boat were replaced by silence. On about the tenth try, one of the girls said, "Could I get in the water with him?" She did, and quietly spoke with him for a few minutes. She then grabbed onto the back of his skis to steady him and hollered, "GO!" He got right up, elbows wobbling, knees shaking, and a huge smile plastered across his face. We could hear the joyful shouts of the girl in the water over the roar of the engine as we sped off.

This high school girl lived out the principles of understanding, imagination, and humility. She understood how hard it is to learn to water-ski. She knew he could learn and encouraged him in that direction. And she stopped yelling at him from the boat. She displayed humility by jumping in the water with him.

This is what we want to say to parents many times. Get in the water. Your child has PO-TENTIAL. He can learn how to ski. He can be aware of his younger sister's feelings. She can learn how to share the load as part of your family. He can make it without drugs and alcohol. She will get through the pain of her father's death. Every adolescent has PO-TENTIAL. As we love them with understanding, imagination, and humility, we call out that God-given potential and urge them on to whom God is creating them to be.

8

Holding Their Hands, Pointing Our Fingers

And let us consider how we may spur one another on toward love and good deeds.

—Hebrews 10:24

Melissa's grandmother, Otie, lived to be 103 years old. Otie was a woman of great wisdom and great strength. She never stopped learning, never stopped rocking in her rocking chair, and never stopped teaching and loving Melissa. She had a profound impact on Melissa's life and faith.

On Otie's one hundredth birthday, which also happened to be Christmas Day, Melissa's family held a birthday party for her. During the party, Melissa walked over to her grandmother's rocking chair to talk to her. "Grandmother, how are you doing?" Melissa asked. "Melissa, come here." She grabbed Melissa's hand tightly and said, "Melissa, I love you. I pray for you every night." She then squinted her piercing blue eyes, took her crooked index finger and pointed it at Melissa. "You behave yourself. Be a good girl."

She held Melissa's hand. She squeezed it as she told Melissa how much she cared for her. Then she pointed her finger and told Melissa how she needed to be living. In holding Melissa's hand *and* pointing her own finger, Otie spurred Melissa on toward love and good deeds.

This chapter is about holding our adolescents' hands and pointing our fingers. The verse in Hebrews says, "let us consider *how* we may spur one another on toward love and good deeds" (emphasis added). Here is what our considering has come up with: following Melissa's grandmother's example, we hold the hands of our adolescents and point our fingers at them. We do both. To only hold their hands would put us in the place of the dove parent we talked about in the introduction. Our children would become arrogant and demanding. To only point our finger would put us in the place of the snake parent. Our children would feel talked down to and criticized. We want to spur our children on toward love and good deeds. When we hold their hands, we engage them. When we point our fingers (as we're holding their hands), we encourage them. To engage and encourage our adolescents is to shape them.

In this chapter, we will examine both. We will look at the power of holding hands and engaging our adolescents. We will also talk about the importance of encouraging them by pointing our fingers. We will then follow the example of a character named Polwarth, and look practically at how the holding of hands and the pointing of fingers work together to bring about a respect that shapes our adolescents.

Holding Their Hands

To hold the hand of our adolescents is to engage them. We recently had breakfast with a dad whose daughters are in high school. As a single father, this dad has been through the ringer with his adolescent daughters, loving them through expulsion, addiction, boyfriend problems, and everything in between. "After all this time, I think I'm finally figuring out this parenting thing," he exuberantly announced to us. "It's all about engaging. Even when they are acting out and telling you they hate you, you can still engage. You can still hug them and say, 'That's okay if you hate me. I love you, anyway.'"

Without intending to, this father defined for us what it means to engage. He talked about two ways to engage:

1) touching our adolescents, when he said "you can still hug them," and

2) telling our adolescents "that's okay if you hate me. I love you, anyway." We can engage our children with physical touch, whether it's a hug or a pat on the shoulder. And we can engage them with the ways that we choose to remind them of our love.

You Can Still Hug Them

While writing this book, we have noticed how God specifically puts things in our paths to illustrate what we're talking about. Last night, we went to a Nickel Creek concert with two of our friends, Pace and June. Two rows in front of us sat a teenager with her mother on one side and her dad on the other. The dad had his arm draped across the back of his daughter's chair. The mother sat turned toward her daughter and was playing with her hair. If these had been parents of a young child, we probably wouldn't have given it a moment's notice. But this was different. We see parents being affectionate with young children every day, but to see parents acting this way with their adolescent children (and adolescent children allowing it) is very rare. It is rare because adolescents don't often even attend concerts with their parents. And it is even more rare because if they did attend a concert with their parents, most adolescents wouldn't think of allowing their parents to touch them in public. We watched for a long time as this sweet family smiled to each other at the warmth that passed between them.

In her book *Comforting One Another*, Karen Mains speaks at length about the significance of physical touch.

> We must begin with the understanding that holding and being held, giving and receiving safe, tender, protective touch is one of the basic needs of human existence. It is indeed, as the studies show, essential to growth, to survival, to well-being.[1]

We all respond to touch. We may be on the verge of tears and finally feel the freedom to cry as a friend puts her arm around us. We can feel the tension drain from our shoulders as we receive a back rub. We remember the comfort of holding our parent's hand as we crossed the street when we were younger.

For adolescents, however, touch can be a double-edged sword. We reach out to touch our adolescents, and they may shrink back. We try to hug them, and they may stand as stiff as a board. "Please don't touch me, Dad." "Get away, Mom."

Does this mean they are exempt from the universal need for touch? *Absolutely not.* It means that developmentally, they are in a state of hyperawareness of their own bodies. They are uncomfortable with their gangly legs, pimply faces, and beginning sense of sexuality. They get "weirded out" when someone other than another teenager tries to reach into their personal comfort zone.

An adolescent girl recently told us of an ongoing argument she has with her mother. She will come home after school, and her mother will want a hug. Rather than standing stiff as a board, this adolescent takes off. She scampers around the house doing her best to evade her mother's embrace. And her mom chases her. Her words to us were, "She drives me crazy. I wish she would stop trying to hug me all the time." The entire time she said these words, however, she was smiling. The knowledge that her mother wanted to hug her did as much for this adolescent as a hug itself. She felt loved.

Because adolescents are so squeamish about touch, it is important that we not approach them in the same way we did when they were younger. Each adolescent is different. A good rule of thumb is to look at their level of comfort and go a step beyond it. If your child cannot stand to ever be touched, a pat on the shoulder can be enough of a reminder of your love.

It is easy, then, to fall into touch being for *us*, rather than for our adolescents. We don't feel connected to our teenagers. We want to reach out and know that they are still there...that they are still the child that we know and love.

So we touch them in a way that says, "I need you to respond to me." This is very different from touch that says, "I love you and want you to respond, but it's your choice." This kind of touch is much harder. We naturally want response. It's when our wanting becomes a demand, however, that our touch can cause damage. Children are perceptive. They pick up on our demand and start to feel that we are dependent on them. As a result, they feel a power that they neither need nor want.

When offered without demand, physical touch can have a profound effect on the lives of our adolescents. As we reach out and touch them, whether it is by patting their shoulder, playing with their hair, or holding their hands, we offer them something of ourselves. We engage them.

Frederick Buechner wrote:

> Through simply touching, more directly than in any other way, we can transmit to each other

something of the power of the life we have inside us. It is no wonder that the laying on of hands has always been a traditional part of healing or that when Jesus was around, "all the crowd sought to touch him" (Luke 6:19). It is no wonder that just the touch of another human being at a dark time can be enough to save the day.[2]

I Love You, Anyway

To say to our adolescents, "I love you, anyway," is to remind them that we care, regardless of how they act. We are giving them the message that no amount of bad behavior, angry words, or rebelliousness can sever our love for them.

How do we do this, especially in light of the fact that their actions are saying to us, "Come close, get away"? They are saying this because they are simultaneously wanting intimacy and independence, which we talked about in Chapter 1. They are also saying this because, deep inside, every child fears being left. For those who have been neglected, adopted, or who have had a parent leave, however, the fear is even stronger.

Teenagers respond to this fear in one of two ways. They may try to sabotage our relationship. This child does everything within their power to make us leave, so they will no longer have to fear our leaving. Another child may try to push us to our limit, just to see how we will respond. Regardless of their circumstances, every child wants to know that we love them enough to stay.

Several years ago, a sixth-grade girl whose parents were divorced described this in her group counseling session.

> I don't understand my dad. He left my mom a long time ago. He says he still loves me and that

it wasn't me he was leaving, it was my mom. But he never calls me and never wants to hang out with me. I guess I feel like he really did leave me. And that, if I made him mad enough, he'd leave me forever. But my mom is really different. I know that I can make her mad and get in trouble and that she'll still love me. She's like a rubber band. I can push and push her, and she'll always come back.

This mom was and still is engaged with her daughter. Her daughter has pushed every limit she has, and her mother has held fast. Holding the hands of our adolescent children tells them not only that we love them, but also that we are committed to them. No matter how hard they try to push, we will not let go.

Pointing Our Fingers

Engaging is essential in our attempts to shape adolescents. Encouragement is equally essential, but not the bland, passive kind of encouragement we often fall into. Rather, we need to use encouragement that speaks directly to the fears and struggles of our adolescents, an encouragement that acknowledges their sin and spurs them on from there toward love and good deeds. We engage our adolescents by holding their hands, but we encourage them by pointing our fingers.

Help! My Child Has Low Self-Esteem

Many of the parents who come into our offices are distraught over the emotions and behaviors of their adolescent children. Their child may be depressed, experimenting with drugs, or spewing anger all over their home. Whatever the symptom, many parents believe the problem to be the same: low self-esteem.

When we hear this, we cringe, not because these parents are wrong, but because they have no idea how right they are. Low self-esteem is as universal as sadness, anger, or fear. If someone does not struggle with low self-esteem, they most likely don't struggle with any emotion. Their heads are probably significantly disconnected from their hearts.

We have a friend who just graduated from high school. She is warm, intelligent, talented, and beautiful. On the outside, she is what every parent would ever want their adolescent child to be like. And she lived her first 18 years with a head that was completely disconnected from her heart. One afternoon in the spring of her senior year, it all came crashing in on her.

> It hadn't been a particularly bad day. But I just felt incredibly overwhelmed. I had a choir performance that night, two tests the next day, and was angry with one of my friends. It was the first time in my life I really remember feeling angry. All of a sudden there was so much of it. I was angry because I was tired of trying to get perfect grades. I was angry because I was tired of trying to be what everyone wanted me to be. I got in my car and started screaming. I screamed out every bad thought I had ever had, every curse word I knew, and everything I hated about myself. Before I knew it, my voice was hoarse, tears were streaming down my face, and I was yelling, "And why did you give me these legs, God?"

The pressure this young woman felt was bound to cause her to blow at some point. Her head finally caught up with her heart. She had spent her entire lifetime trying to get things right. She would be the last person anyone would ever guess would have self-esteem problems. But like every other teenager, it was there all the time, brewing in the depths of her heart.

This is not to say that there are not extreme cases of low self-esteem that need to be dealt with. What we are saying is that there is a baseline level of low self-esteem that every one of us experiences, including, and sometimes particularly, our adolescents.

I Am a Mess!

One of the unique aspects of Daystar is that every child there, at one time or another, has heard the phrase, "You are a mess." We typically use the word mess, rather than sinner, because they are better able to connect with it. But we are essentially saying the same thing. We are saying what they know to be true. We are saying, "We see you. We know that you are capable of hurting other people, hurting yourself, and hurting God. And we know that you have, at one time or another, done all three."

At our summer camps, meals are a very important time. The kids help prepare the meals and get very excited when they get to help with certain meals that are camp favorites. One of these meals is pancakes. Pancakes typically take a long time to make because the kids make blueberry, banana, and chocolate chip, and even go as far as to make them in certain shapes. So we sometimes wait up to two hours for pancakes. One of these pancake mornings, we were upstairs meeting as a staff when one of the interns flew into Melissa's room and said, "Y'all need to come downstairs. You're not going to believe what's happening."

What was happening was that the kids had turned on themselves by splitting off into groups and talking about other people at camp. They were talking negatively about different groups and types of people. Now this may not sound unusual from a group of teenagers. But it is something we are strongly against at Daystar camp.

So we walked downstairs, where the first few kids in line had just sat down with their much-anticipated pancakes. Melissa loudly said, "Stop! I don't want you to take another bite. This table is representative of the table of the Lord, and we are not coming to His table having hurt each other. I want each one of you to get up and find whomever you have offended. I want you to ask their forgiveness and get back in line. Then before you get your pancakes, I want you to say these words: 'I am a mess.'"

We walked to the front of the line, admitted that we were messes, too, and received our pancakes. We then walked back upstairs to the repeated words "I am a mess, I am a mess, I am a mess" as the kids received their pancakes.

Some parents might be shocked to hear our "I am a mess" lesson. They might ask: "My child has low self-esteem, and you just told them that they are a mess?"

Yes, we did. Actually, when we call teenagers a mess, their most common response is to smile. We believe that this is true encouragement. We believe our friend who just graduated from high school needed to hear this message long ago. Somewhere inside of them, every adolescent knows that they are a mess. True encouragement acknowledges the mess that they are, and spurs them on to something greater.

Get on Out There!

When we were in New York after the attack on the World Trade Center, we were fortunate to be able to spend some time with a few of the firemen. One of these men had been close to the beloved fire department chaplain, Father Mychal Judge.

Father Judge was one of the first heroes to fall that day in September. He was a man respected and loved by every firefighter he knew, including the one who told us this story.

> I remember one time, I was asked to speak to a group of about 100 new recruits. I was standing beside Father and I told him I didn't want to go out there. I was really scared. He said to me, "You have walked into countless fires without ever looking back. You have saved lives. Do you mean to tell me you're afraid to speak to a few firemen? Get on out there," he said as he actually shoved me onto the stage.

Father Judge was demonstrating true encouragement. He spoke to his friend's fears. He pointed his finger by shoving him onto the stage and saying, "Get on out there."

> *And let us consider how we may spur one another on toward love and good deeds. Let us not give up meeting together, as some are in the habit of doing, but let us encourage one another—and all the more as you see the Day approaching.*
>
> —HEBREWS 10:24-25

The definition of encouragement is to inspire courage or strength in preparation for a hard task. En-courage. Adolescents are already in the middle of a hard task: growing up. They know well that they are messes. They know they fail, and much of their low self-esteem comes from their own frustration with their messiness. As we point our fingers at them, we echo the words of Father Judge. "I see you. I know you are a mess, but you are capable of so much more. Now, get on out there!"

The Power of Held Hands and Pointed Fingers

> Remember, God wants us to confess and cease from sin so we can be free of it and enjoy the greatest freedom of all—joy. His desire is that we live in the light, which is why he prods us to face our darkness. A recurring theme here, and a relentlessly recurring theme in the Bible, is that to experience the miracle of God's grace we must continually face the mess within. One leads to the other.[3]
>
> —REBECCA MANLEY PIPPERT

If we are not aware of our sin, we are not aware that we need a Savior. Adolescents know that they fail. They respond with a smile when we tell them that they are a mess. This is precisely the reason adolescence is the time that many people enter into a relationship with Christ.

This is where our holding their hands and pointing our fingers becomes very important. Many adolescents are in hiding. They do not understand what they know to be true about themselves and our attempts to raise their low self-esteem. So their response is to take their messiness and hide it. If we knew what was happening inside of them, we might no longer believe in them. They might disappoint us or even cause us to want to leave.

When we see an adolescent struggling, it is easy to think, "I just want my child to feel good about himself." To feel good is for them to know they don't have to hide. When we see them for who they are and love them anyway, they are freed to acknowledge their sin. As we hold their hands and point our fingers, we communicate that no amount of messiness will sever our love. We communicate the miracle and the mystery of the cross. We shape them by spurring them on toward love and good deeds.

Practical Polwarth

How do we actually walk this out? As parents, teachers, counselors, and youth directors, how do we teach by holding our adolescents hands and pointing our fingers? This is where the respect takes center stage. We respect our adolescents by moving beyond their potential for sin and reminding them of their potential for greatness. Adolescents feel respected when they know that we see them as they are and still believe they are capable of great things. We show respect for them in the ways that we shape or teach them.

In his book *The Curate's Awakening*, George MacDonald introduces a character named Polwarth, who could be considered the quintessential adolescent teacher (even though there wasn't an adolescent in the book). MacDonald writes: "Polwarth did not want to say or explain too much, for he did not want to weaken by presentation the force of a truth which, in discovery, would have its full effect."[4] Let's follow his example. Polwarth (1) didn't want to say or explain too much, (2) didn't want to weaken the truth by presentation, and (3) recognized the importance of discovering truth.

1) Don't say too much.

By the time our children have reached the age of 12 or 13, they are well-acquainted with our voices. They know what we believe about most things and probably could provide our answer to almost every question that could be asked.

We meet with parents and their adolescent children often for family counseling. During these meetings, it is not at all uncommon to watch as the teenager's eyes become glassy with daydreams as the parents try to talk to them about their concerns. This is not only because they have already heard a great deal of what we are going to say; it is also because we have a tendency to explain until we feel like they truly understand.

A huge complaint of teenagers is that adults repeat themselves over and over. We do this because we think they are not listening. We are exactly right. They hear probably 10 percent of what we say to them in any given soliloquy. Many of us give these soliloquies every time we have a concern about what our children have said or done. We speak often with parents about choosing battles. It is equally important to choose words, and to be short and direct in the words we choose.

2) Don't weaken the truth by its presentation.

Teaching adolescents is drastically different than teaching young children. Most of our teaching with young children is done with us standing in front of them, speaking to them. With adolescents, it is important that we involve them. We do this by valuing and respecting their opinions. During our devotional times at camp, the kids feel completely free to ask questions and respond to what Melissa is teaching.

One year at camp, there were about 30 of us gathered in the living room of the lakehouse owned by Sissy's family. Melissa was teaching on hope, and how Christ's death on the cross offers us that hope. In front of all her peers, one of the girls who tended toward shyness raised her hand. "Melissa, everyone always gets so emotional when they talk about the cross. I'm just not sure I believe in any of it."

This was a tremendous step for this young girl to take. She took a great risk in raising her hand and saying something that could potentially cause controversy. And she was trying to find what she believed to be true for herself, not just because she had always been told it.

As we said before, adolescence is an important time in our childrens' journeys toward faith. It is a time when they naturally ask and wonder. As we help them feel free to ask questions, as we involve them in our teaching, they take more interest. They feel engaged.

If you have family devotionals with your children, ask your teenager to teach one evening. If you are a youth minister, pull your kids in to take on more leadership roles. The more that adolescents take ownership and feel free to be who they are in the midst of our teaching, the more they receive from it.

3) Help them discover truth.

Many nights at camp, we do not tell the kids that it is time for worship. The staff simply sits together in the living room and starts singing. Our hearts are always moved as the kids wander in, either by themselves or in small groups. They wander in not because we shout out, "COME ON, EVERYONE!!! WE'RE STARTING WORSHIP!" They come in because they feel invited. They have a choice. Without fail, these nights are always our most powerful nights of worship.

In the same way, we never force high school students to participate in group counseling. We usually ask them (or strongly urge them) to try it three times, and then to make their own choice. We have found that the kids who are forced to come give and receive less from group than those who are given a choice. When they are given a choice, they feel they have made the discovery.

A mom who has been involved with Daystar for years faced a dilemma involving this type of choice. All three of her children have gone through counseling at Daystar, and she has been very involved in our moms' group herself. Several years ago, Sissy went to speak to her about her daughter. Sissy said: "I feel like it's time you let her make her own choice about groups. I think she ends up resenting it more than receiving from it. She may quit and never come back. Or, she may realize what group does mean to her and decide to stay. We will pray strongly for the latter. But it is time that she made that choice."

After many tears, this mom allowed her daughter to make her own choice. She was afraid her daughter would reject not only counseling but what it represented: making good choices, having people with whom she was accountable, and the journey toward her own faith.

Her daughter did quit group. But several years later, she called Melissa. "Things have gotten really hard at school, and I was wondering if I could come back to Daystar."

This young woman now has a star tattooed on her back (quite an unusual representation of what Daystar has meant to her). A high school senior, she says that one of the things she will miss the most next year when she is in college is her Daystar group.

This is the power of choice. When any of us are forced to participate in something, our resentment chokes out what we could potentially receive. Adolescents particularly are caught up in perpetual power struggles. As adults we need to maintain some of the power struggles and assert our leadership. But there are some times that we can give our children choices, even when the choice seems to be a great risk. When they make a choice on their own, they receive and give with much more meaning. They experience the joy of discovery.

An Unusual Encouragement

When we are teaching adolescents, it is imperative that we start where they are. They are experiencing strong emotions that they don't know what to do with. They are searching for God at much deeper levels. They are moving past black-and-white thinking, and our teaching needs to challenge them at that place. Encourage your adolescents to talk about their struggles. Don't try to make their disappointment go away. Use it to talk about how God redeems even our pain. Share your own stories of struggles. When we speak only to where we think teenagers should be, we miss them. But when we speak to where they are, we engage them.

Almost 20 years ago, Melissa was in a little corner store in Kentucky. Above the counter, taped with scraps of torn masking tape, was a small cardboard sign. On it were these words:

> Lost, Black Cat
> Answers to the Name of Tom
> He's Ugly, But I Love Him

Within the words on that sign the Gospel of Christ lies hidden. We could just as easily substitute our own names.

> Lost, White Women
> Answer to the Names of Melissa and Sissy
> They're Ugly, But I Love Them

Melissa told this story at the eleventh- and twelfth-grade camp this summer. The kids loved it and went back to it time and time again as they shared throughout the week. They already identify with the lost black cat named Tom. They know their own sin, messiness, and ugliness. Their fear is that no one will put up a sign or come looking for them.

As we hold our adolescents' hands and point our fingers, we speak to that fear. We touch them where they are. We let them know that we see them, we still love them, and we're going to give them a good, strong shove toward all the love and good deeds found in the cross of Christ.

9

A Thankful Heart

Satan can't live in my thankful heart,
My thankful heart, My thankful heart
Satan can't live in my thankful heart.
My thankful heart's full.

—A SONG WRITTEN BY THE DAYSTAR KIDS
TO THE TUNE OF "DON'T THROW YOUR
TRASH IN MY BACKYARD"

If there is one statement that kids from Daystar camp remember, it is this:

Satan can't live in a thankful heart.

For the past four years, this statement has been a foundation of our worship. Almost every night after we have finished singing and before Melissa starts teaching, we spend time reflecting on what we have been thankful for on that particular day.

Gratitude is not something that naturally flows out of teenagers. These teenagers have spent an entire day on the lake and are tired and often frustrated. Many of the kids at our camps are going through some type of loss or difficulty. Their parents are going through a divorce. They have lost a family member. They have lived a lifetime of being left out by other kids. These kids, particularly, are not accustomed to being thankful. And understandably so. Many of them are confused, depressed, and angry. But even in the midst of the struggle, we still believe firmly in this statement:

Satan can't live in a thankful heart.

We ask, "So, who has something they were thankful for today?"

It usually starts slowly. After a few minutes of looking around the room, one person will raise their hand.

- "I'm thankful for John, because when I fell off of the banana, he helped me back on."

- "I'm thankful for Carol. When I was lying on my bed feeling a little homesick, she came in to check on me."

- "I'm thankful for Betsie, because we had so much fun together making breakfast."

And on and on until every person in the room has contributed something to the gratitude pot.

Thus this song was composed by ninth- and tenth-grade campers last year to go along with our Thanksgiving meal. (We not only have Christmas in July, but Thanksgiving as well.) While one half of the group was singing "Turkey, ham and stuffing, stuffing, stuffing" the others were singing "Satan can't live in my thankful heart."

We believe that gratitude is an essential part of shaping adolescents. That is why, in our camps and in our counseling, we go back to this statement over and over. And that is why we have built a chapter around this very statement: *Satan can't live in a thankful heart.*

In this chapter, we will examine our hearts and the change that gratitude brings about in them. We will look at our natural hearts and how we often prevent gratitude from fulfilling its mission. We will talk about the importance of a receptive heart and how to allow our lives to be filled with the gifts God has given us. And finally, we will look at a responsive heart, both how God has called us to respond and how we can encourage our adolescent children to do the same.

A Natural Heart

In the first few days of camp, our time of thankfulness seems to go particularly slowly. This is because thankfulness is not the typical dialect of adolescence. If we were to listen in on a phone conversation between our teenage child and one of their friends (which we are by no means suggesting), these are the things we would typically hear:

- "What was Susan thinking wearing that outfit today?"

- "Brian thinks he's cool just because he got that new car."

- "All my dad ever does is tell me what to do."

- "I wish my mom would quit asking me questions."

Not a great deal of gratitude in the words of most teenagers. There are definitely exceptions, but our experience has been that the exceptions feel more like outcasts. We talked in Chapter 1 about the imaginary audience and the exaggerated importance of peers. With this kind of pressure, fitting in takes highest priority. The cost of being different is entirely too much to pay for most teenagers.

Unfortunately, adolescents are not aware of the real cost found in this kind of attitude. Complaining and criticizing put any of us on a downward spiral. The end of that spiral is the very bottom of ourselves. We lose our sense of life, enjoyment, and thankfulness. We end up depressed, bitter, or angry, and many times all of the above.

But we believe that underneath the complaints and the criticisms, there is something even deeper that robs us of gratitude. It applies to our adolescents and to us as well.

While talking through this chapter, the two of us realized that we approach (and mostly avoid) gratitude in entirely different ways. These ways have to do with our personalities, which are often completely opposite.

There is a well-known saying that "Life is hard, but God is good." We are going to place ourselves at either end of the "Life is hard, God is good" continuum. We believe that every one of us, adults and adolescents, can be found somewhere in between.

Life Is Hard

Melissa is what we would call a "muller." She loves to mull and think through every available option. It took her almost a year to decide what kind of dog she wanted to buy, and then two months to name her. She has a million ideas, going in every possible direction. She is a visionary, constantly looking at the big picture. Melissa sees the reality of life, but she is not a pessimist. She knows and can deeply empathize with others' pain. She is fully aware of the fact that life is hard. Melissa lives life with a deep awareness of the hearts and needs of other people. This is the upside.

The downside of this particular end of the continuum is the tendency to get stuck. If Melissa were writing this book by herself, there would be great depth and wisdom, but the book would never actually be finished. It would never be good enough, according to her.

An adolescent on the *life is hard* end tends toward depression. He is aware of his own inadequacies and failures. His eyes have been opened to the pain in his own life and others. But he is stuck. The challenge for this adolescent is to move past the pain to an understanding that God truly is good.

God Is Good

Sissy leans toward thankfulness much more easily. She has a deep need to enjoy life, and does so often. Her enthusiasm invites others to enjoy life as well. She possesses a warmth and energy that make others feel loved. Sissy makes quick and confident decisions and appears very self-assured. If Sissy were writing this book alone, it would be finished in two months but would only contain a fraction of its depth.

The negative part of this personality can be its lack of awareness. This person often skims the surface of life, easily maintaining their positive outlook precisely because of this skimming. They find themselves much more sympathetic with another's pain than empathetic.

For an adolescent, this personality often pretends and sometimes believes that everything is wonderful. Other kids may respect her but feel that she is somehow unapproachable. This teenager lives life either alone or with others who are equally happy. The challenge for this adolescent is to acknowledge that life is hard and God is still good.

The power is found in the two ends coming together. *Once we have become aware and have acknowledged that life is hard, we know with much more depth and conviction that God is good.*

A Receptive Heart

> *Every good and perfect gift is from above, coming down from the Father of the heavenly lights, who does not change like shifting shadows.*
>
> —JAMES 1:17

How do we move out of our natural hearts toward genuine gratitude? How do we help our adolescents make the same move?

Gratitude begins with a Giver. We must first, ourselves, believe that the Giver is good and can be trusted. As we learn to live our lives trusting in the Giver, He creates in us receptive hearts. We then are freed to help our children experience genuine gratitude as well.

Our Receptive Hearts

A man we know told us about Christmas at his house. He talked about the thought and energy that he and his siblings pour into buying gifts for their mother. All the children and grandchildren open their gifts, with the grandmother stoically watching over them. When everyone is finished, the focus shifts as she opens each of her gifts. As she is unwrapping the packages, the giver will often say, "Mom, I thought you would like this because…." They will try to make the gift more attractive to her. But most of the time, she simply unwraps it and puts it aside. Sometimes she will even go as far as to say, "Well, why in the world did you buy me that? I sure don't need it." Whether she says these words or not, it is obvious that the gift has not become hers. She will return it the first chance she gets.

This woman obviously finds it difficult to receive. She may be stuck in the fact that *life is hard*, so why would anyone give her any gift that would make a difference? Or, she may be looking at life through *God is good* lenses and not acknowledge that she even has a need.

Either way, receiving is difficult for all of us. It is both frightening and humbling. Ultimately, receiving involves trust. It involves trusting that there is One who loves us and knows us intimately. It is trusting that He knows and will bring to fruition what is for our ultimate good. And it is trusting that He also gives good gifts in ways we might not expect. It may be a new friend who shares truth with us. It may be a financial gift from someone who sees our need. Or, it may be a gift of forgiveness from someone we have harmed.

As we begin to have this kind of trust, our hearts become receptive and move toward genuine gratitude. Thomas Merton wrote:

> To be grateful is to recognize the Love of God in everything He has given us—and He has given us everything. Every breath we draw is a gift of His love, every moment of existence is a gift of grace, for it brings with it immense graces from Him. Gratitude therefore takes nothing for granted, is never unresponsive, is constantly awakening to new wonder and to praise of the goodness of God. For the grateful man knows that God is good, not by hearsay but by experience. And that is what makes all the difference.[1]

Their Receptive Hearts

Our experience of gratitude makes all the difference for us, according to Merton. It also makes a tremendous difference in the lives of our children. Gratitude is contagious. When we live our lives in appreciation to God and others, our children will also reap the benefits.

How else can we help our children have receptive hearts? How can we help them experience gratitude for themselves?

Let us answer that question in reverse. In the same ways that our lack of trust can prevent us from receiving, the ways that we respond to our children can prevent them from receiving, as well.

Teenagers' eyes are being opened to the realities of life. They are discovering their own fears, limitations, and failures. They are also experiencing deeper levels of longing, desire, and need than they ever have before. As adults, our response to these discoveries is of the utmost importance.

We see parents respond in two different directions.

The Protective Parent

The first parent steps in to protect their children. This is the parent who calls the cheerleading sponsor when their child doesn't make cheerleading and convinces them to add one more person to the squad. This is the parent who stays up until three in the morning to finish the project *for* their child (who is usually sleeping) rather than *with* the child. This parent has wonderful motives. He loves his children and does not want them to hurt, fail, or be in need.

The consequence of the protective parent is that his children often do not learn cause and effect. Rather than protecting them from difficulties, he prevents them from learning valuable lessons. He prevents them from coming face-to-face with the fact that life is hard. In effect, he arrests what is naturally happening within adolescents. He prevents his children from experiencing the longings, the pain, and the disappointments. In turn, he also prevents them from any kind of deeper need. His children do not experience the joy of receiving because they never become aware of their own need.

We recently met with parents of a freshman in college. A few months before, this young man had bought a brand new car. He did it without his parents' permission or help. They didn't even know he was doing it. Because his family had connections in the bank, getting a loan was no problem. What was a problem, however, was following through with the payment. When he couldn't make his car payment on time, the bank called his father. His father left work immediately and went to pay the bill. "What was I going to do? Let the bank repossess his car?"

Actually, yes. Let the bank repossess his car. He would see his need much more clearly. In other cases, grieve with your daughter over the fact that she didn't make cheerleading. The sadness can turn her toward Christ like nothing ever has before. Or, allow yourself to feel with your son what it would be like to fail the seventh grade. When he has pulled through at the end of the semester, he will experience genuine gratitude.

Understand. Have compassion. Protect when you need to, but don't prevent. Don't shield your child from the difficulties of life. God designed adolescence the way He did for a purpose. Love and support them through those lessons. Don't prevent them from experiencing the very things that can cause their hearts to be receptive.

The Permissive Parent

The second parent is one that we will call the permissive parent. She believes lessons need to be learned the hard way. She stands by and allows her children to duke it out with each other. When her children get into difficulties in school, she tells them to work it out themselves. When she receives the call from the police, she allows her child to stay in juvenile hall as long as it takes. She supports her children but rarely intervenes.

The consequences of the permissive parent can potentially be even more damaging than those of the protective parent. Without any intervention, our children can get themselves into problems that move beyond teaching them lessons to actually damaging their hearts.

One permissive parent we know was married to a man who was abusive. He and his son would get into fights frequently. The mom believed that if she were to step in, she would prevent them from working anything out on their own. "It's their relationship. They need to deal with it. I'm only going to confuse the issue." The fights escalated until they became physical.

The son of this permissive parent now has a terrible time receiving. He does not trust that he will be protected and believes the only answer is to always protect himself.

Permissive parents come at it from an entirely different direction but still can prevent their children from having receptive hearts. Their children never experience gratitude because they never let down their guards long enough to recognize good gifts.

The Permissive, Then Protective Parent

We believe that parents who help their children develop receptive hearts are those that are permissive to a point, and then step in to protect. They see the importance of the lessons learned in difficulties but have no problem intervening when the need arises.

A friend of ours in high school was having difficulty getting along with her soccer coach. He yelled at the girls regularly during practices and was demeaning and critical. This student went several times to talk to her coach, who only berated her in response. She then went to the headmaster. He called the coach in and talked to him about the problem. The coach still didn't change. Finally, the girl's mom felt that it was time to step in. She called a meeting with the headmaster and coach and threatened to go to the school board.

This high school student confronted the problem. She tried several times to deal with it herself. But nothing was changing. Her spirit was beginning to be damaged as a result. Her mom took action when necessary but still allowed her daughter to go through the difficulty and learn the lesson.

When we allow our children to experience failures, disappointments, longings, and desires, we give them the opportunity to truly experience God. As they come to know His goodness for themselves, their hearts can become receptive and they can begin to taste genuine gratitude.

A Responsive Heart

We have moved from natural hearts to receiving hearts. Receiving, however, is only a portion of gratitude. We can receive a gift, and even enjoy it, and never respond with gratitude to the giver. To receive is to feel gratitude. To respond is to walk that gratitude out. To respond is a choice, but it's a choice we can make in obedience to God's command.

> *In everything, give thanks; for this is God's will for you in Christ Jesus.*
> —1 THESSALONIANS 5:18 NASB

A Choice to Obey

Several summers ago, Melissa taught on the Psalms to a group of high school students. Actually, what she did was have each of them write their own Psalm. She went through several different Psalms in the Bible and came up with a framework for the kids to follow. They were told to: (1) Call God by name; (2) Ask God for something they thought they deserved; (3) Tell God why they thought they deserved it; (4) Call down vengeance on those who already have it; and (5) Give thanks to God.

For all of us writing, the switch from four to five was very difficult. It felt unnatural and fake. We have heard the same responses from some of the Daystar kids when we talk about the importance of being thankful.

- "Sometimes, I just don't feel like it. What am I supposed to do then?"

- "I'm really angry at my mom. I don't feel thankful for anything."

- "I'm the whole reason our team lost. What do I have to be thankful about?"

The Psalms are littered with gratitude. They are also littered with pain, disappointment, and longing. The

Psalmists always express their feelings, and they always move toward gratitude. They make a very important choice in response to a very important command.

Henri Nouwen wrote:

> The choice for gratitude rarely comes without some real effort. But each time I make it, the next choice is a little easier, a little freer, a little less self-conscious. Because every gift I acknowledge reveals another and another, until finally even the most normal, obvious, and seemingly mundane event or encounter proves to be filled with grace.[2]

Our adolescents have the ability to make the same type of choice. No matter how much pain they are in, no matter what the other kids are doing, they can still choose to respond. We want our adolescents to share their feelings, but we don't want them to become victims of those feelings. They can still choose to respond out of obedience.

A Friendly Nudge

Several years ago, Sissy was meeting with a young woman who definitely falls into the *life is hard* category. She had been struggling with depression for months and was meeting weekly with Sissy for individual counseling appointments. One week she came in experiencing total despair. She cried for the first 45 minutes of the session, talking about how nothing in her life was good. Her parents didn't love her, her friends weren't there for her, she couldn't do anything right, and on from there. She was in a tremendous downward spiral. After letting her talk through all of her feelings, Sissy spoke up.

"Okay, stop. You left reality behind quite some time ago. You are a very bright, loved, enjoyable, delightful person, and it's time you recognized that. The voices you are hearing are not truth. They are lies. And things are not going to get better until you silence those lies. Satan can't live in a thankful heart, and somehow he's having a heyday in yours. Tell me what you're thankful for."

"I can't. I don't know anything."

"Yes, you do. Tell me something."

"No, I can't think of anything."

Their voices were growing louder and louder until the young woman finally said,

"OKAY. I'M THANKFUL FOR THIS TREE IN YOUR OFFICE THAT IS SUPPOSED TO GIVE OFF OXYGEN SO THAT WE CAN BREATHE BUT CAN'T BECAUSE IT'S FAKE!!!"

This young woman made a difficult choice. In the midst of a great deal of pain, she chose to respond with gratitude (and a little sarcasm). Our obedience and the obedience of our children should not be dictated by our feelings. In his book *A Long Obedience in the Same Direction*, Eugene Peterson talks about the discrepancy we may feel between our hearts and God's command. "Act your gratitude. Pantomime your thanks. You will become that which you do."

Whether we feel thankful or not, we can choose to live out God's command. In doing so, we are fulfilling God's will and silencing the voice of the accuser. *Satan can't live in a thankful heart.*

> *When an evil spirit comes out of a man, it goes through arid places seeking rest and does not find it. Then it says, "I will return to the house I left." When it arrives, it finds the house unoccupied, swept clean and put in order. Then it goes and takes with it seven other spirits more wicked than itself, and they go in and live there. And*

> *the final condition of that man is worse than the*
> *first.*
> —MATTHEW 12:43-45

Gratitude is not natural for any of us...neither us, as adults, nor our adolescent children. We spend a great deal of time sweeping our houses clean and putting them in order. We read parenting books (like this one), attend seminars, and try to make sure we have quality time with our family. But all the knowledge and involvement in the world cannot bring about a change of heart. As Merton said, it is gratitude that makes a difference in our lives. It is gratitude that makes a difference in the lives of our children. As we learn to trust in a God that gives good gifts, we open our hearts to receive. And as we receive and experience the goodness of God for ourselves, we respond with genuine gratitude.

The same holds true for our children. Gratitude makes all the difference. It is worship in a daily way. It is the culmination of shaping and the springboard for the next section of our book, strengthening.

Satan can't live in a thankful heart. When our hearts are full of gratitude, they are exactly that...filled. Satan has no room or place to bother us. The voices of dread and despair are silenced. We are freed to experience and receive from God with even greater depth. Gratitude begets further gratitude, and we all reap the benefits.

Part Four

Strengthen

Strengthen

Yet, O Lord, you are our Father. We are the clay, you are the potter; we are all the work of your hand.

—Isaiah 64:8

In the lives of our teenagers, we are the potter's assistants. As His assistants, we have watched as their hearts have been softened. We have stood beside Him and even joined our hands with His as He has continued to shape them into who He is creating them to be.

In the previous section, we examined what shaping looks like in the lives of our adolescents, and our role in the process. We looked at how to love our children with understanding, imagination, and humility as we remind them of their PO-TENTIAL. We talked about spurring them on toward love and good deeds by simultaneously holding their hands and pointing our fingers. And finally, we looked at the importance of gratitude. We discussed the power of gratitude in our own hearts and how that helps to lead our children to have thankful hearts of their own.

So the shaping has begun. What now? Unfortunately, this is where many of us believe that the work of loving and parenting our teenagers is finished. We develop a good, foundational relationship with them. We help them to both know the Lord and understand better who He is creating them to be. And then we sit back and breathe a sigh of relief.

But the process is not yet over. The clay has been softened. It has even been shaped into the vision God has given us for that particular piece of clay. But there is one more thing that must be done. The clay must be strengthened. It must be put into the oven for the heat to do its final work of solidifying the piece. If not, it will chip, flake, and fall apart in its use.

What does it mean to help solidify the work being done in our adolescents? How does strengthening take place in their lives? In much the same way as it does in our own. In this next section, we will describe the significance of purpose in the lives of our teenagers.

As our children come to believe that they make a difference, they begin to have a sense of purpose. Purpose acts to solidify all the softening and shaping that has already taken place. It serves to strengthen their faith and their own sense of confidence in who God is creating them to be.

10

Bridge of Hope

— ⌒ —

Only a larger purpose—one that is for each of us personal and passionate—can inspire us to heights we know we could never reach on our own.[1]

—OS GUINNESS

She came to Daystar after being released from the adolescent psychiatric unit at Vanderbilt Hospital. She dressed in black, wore her long hair practically covering her face, and kept her head down. She had attempted suicide, and when she was admitted to the hospital she was diagnosed with depression. As with so many of our teenagers, Melissa felt that groups at Daystar could do her a world of good.

Melissa was right. After approximately a month of individual counseling, this 15-year-old girl became a part of a high school counseling group. Over the course of the next few months, she was loved, enjoyed, confronted, and encouraged by her peers. Her hair gradually fell away from her face, her head lifted, and her beauty began to emerge. She was softening.

The following summer, this young woman attended a Christian camp for girls where she served on kitchen duty.

While there, she encountered Christ. For the first time she could remember, she turned her life over to God and experienced true hope. At that point, God began to shape her into a masterpiece of beauty.

This young woman is now in her early twenties. Last year at Christmas, she had breakfast with Sissy. They talked about her life now and her life then and about the strengthening that took place inside her during a very memorable group counseling session.

> Do you know what I remember the most from my time at Daystar? It was the year after I had accepted Christ at camp. I was a junior in high school, and doing so much better. One of the girls in our group was really struggling with depression. She talked for a long time about the hopelessness and despair she was feeling. And then she looked up at me. I will never forget her words. She said, "Your growth over this last year has blown me away. It has been such an example to me. Who you are now shows me who I can be. You are like a bridge of hope to me, stretching from where I am now to where I can be."

As you can imagine, these words profoundly impacted this high school junior. They impacted her so much that several years later, she decided she wanted her parents to take the money they would have used for Christmas gifts for her and give it to Daystar. She said she wanted others to experience the same healing she had during her time with us.

A significant part of her healing took place in that one group. She was given a glimpse of the impact that her life and journey had on another person. She was told that she made a difference...that she had purpose.

This is the reason we have groups at Daystar. One of the founding principles of Daystar Counseling Ministries is that kids impact other kids. Because of this, groups have a tremendous ability to affect members in either very positive or very negative ways. This is the danger of peer pressure. And this is the power of a peer group moving in a positive direction.

The director of a well-known counseling ministry from another city once asked us about our groups. "I just don't understand how you get your groups to actually work. We keep trying, but the kids either lose interest, or they seem to drag each other down. Parents have complained that it seems like their kids feel worse when they leave group than they did before they came."

We would love to say that our secret is the incredibly wise, well-equipped counselors we have on staff. (We do have a staff that is very gifted and for whom we are both deeply thankful.) We would love to say that we offer programs that inspire and astound the kids involved in our groups. (We do have some great programs, but they are not the answer, either.) Our secret lies in the kids themselves.

At Daystar, any child who participates in a group earns the right to be in that group. He has to be willing to look another child in the eye, call him by name, and not make fun of anyone. We do this because we want groups to be one of the safe places we talked about in Chapter 4. We also do it because we want every child in our groups to feel they have a purpose. Each child has something that he can give. Not only do we want them to know they have something to give, but we want them to know we expect them to give. We have discovered that the more a teenager is willing to give to a group, the more they receive back from that group. The result is a sense of confidence and commitment to the group they would not have otherwise.

So each of our groups has what we would refer to as our "nucleus." Members of the nucleus are not kids who are perfect. They are not even necessarily kids you would choose to lead a group. But they *are* kids, like the young girl in the story above, who are willing to give of themselves to each other. They *are* kids who know and have experienced a sense of purpose in their own lives. They know they make a difference. They are the reasons our groups work, and they are really the heart of the ministry of Daystar.

In this chapter, we are going to examine the need for purpose in the lives of our adolescents. We will look at kids who have lost their sense of purpose: kids who are bored, tired, lifeless, and empty. Based on a verse in 2 Timothy, we will talk about how to help our teenagers pursue purpose. And finally, we will discuss what purpose brings about in the lives of our children.

A Lack of Purpose

A majority of adolescents today would say that they are bored. When asked if they enjoy something, their answer will often be, "It's okay." When asked if they would like to do something, their answer will often be, "Whatever."

Many teenagers walk through life more as spectators than those who are actually participants. As adults, we devote a great deal of time trying to entertain them. We sign them up for any activity we think they might enjoy. We make sure we have games that include enough antics to keep them interested in our youth groups. We are ever seeking to hold their attention and their happiness.

We can't. It simply doesn't work. We end up wearing ourselves out with all the driving and entertaining and clowning. As a result we are exhausted, and they are still bored.

We would take it even a step further and say that many of today's adolescents are more than just bored. Depending on their style, they are often lifeless, tired, or empty.

Good Kids Feel Lifeless

As a teenager, Sissy was the quintessential good kid. She was kind to others (except in the mornings, her dad would say). She excelled in school. She was president of most of the clubs and organizations in which she was involved. She made good choices and was a part of a very sweet, caring group of friends who were Christians and were also good. She was model pledge of her sorority and many would say a model teenager.

But on the inside, she was lifeless. She was doing her best to avoid anger, sadness, and conflict. Creativity and passion were words that were foreign to her. She had the appearance of a cardboard cutout in a music store with no depth behind it.

Busy Kids Are Tired

One boy we know is incredibly busy. He tries to find his purpose in success, and avoids failure. He is an honor student. He volunteers with his church. He is the center for his high school football team. He has a part-time job at a neighborhood grocery store. And he still somehow manages to balance a very full social schedule. How does he do it? Well, he doesn't do it very well. Many weeks he comes into group 20 minutes late, exhausted, and in tears. "I feel like I'm just wandering around from place to place. I'm doing so many things, but I'm not doing anything well. It just seems like none of it really matters. I feel like I just want to give up."

Fun Kids Feel Empty

Melissa was a fun kid. With her dry, witty sense of humor, she was often the life of the party. Wherever she was, there were other people and lots of laughter. Whenever she was with others, she was trying. She was trying to make them laugh, trying to make them feel good, trying to keep everyone happy. Melissa, on the inside, felt empty. She tried to find her purpose in making others laugh and enjoy themselves. But it didn't work for long. The emptiness, along with a feeling of loneliness, always returned.

Rebellious Kids Are Bored

According to his parents, Kevin doesn't know how to be anything but rebellious. "Anything we ask him to do, he does the opposite. We tell him he's grounded. He says he doesn't care. We threaten to take away his car, and he says he'll walk. We have no idea what to do with him. He doesn't seem to care about anything."

Kevin does care, but his care is buried way down deep beneath his boredom. He is looking for excitement, and the way he has found it is by getting into trouble, whether it is by shoplifting or vandalizing private property. His purpose seems to be found in taking risks, even though the risks are foolish.

Good kids, busy kids, fun kids, and rebellious kids are all looking for a sense of purpose. They all want to know that their lives have meaning. They are all asking the same questions, even though they are asking them in entirely different ways.

- "Does my life make a difference?"

- "Will anyone miss me if I'm not here?"

- "Do I count?"

- "Does it matter that I'm alive?"

- "Does anyone really care about me?"

Many teenagers today are bored, tired, lifeless, and empty. They are missing their sense of purpose. As kids move into adulthood, they are looking for clues that their lives have meaning. As Os Guinness wrote:

It is often said that there are three requirements for a fulfilling life. The first two—a clear sense of personal identity and a strong sense of personal mission—are rooted in the third: a deep sense of life's meaning.[2]

This is where we come in. Teenagers need to know they make a difference. They long for purpose and want to feel that they can be a bridge of hope to another. But being teenagers, they often are not going to seek out this purpose for themselves. As adults who love adolescents, we can help them find meaning in their lives. We can help them in the pursuit of purpose.

Pursuing Purpose

Now flee from youthful lusts and pursue righteousness, faith, love and peace, with those who call on the Lord from a pure heart.

—2 TIMOTHY 2:22 NASB

The words from Paul to Timothy echo the same words we would like to say to our teenage children.

1) "Flee from..."

To flee means to run. We don't just think of fleeing as running, though, as in a race. We think of fleeing as running wildly. It is running from something toward something else, with a wild abandon.

What is Timothy told to flee? Youthful lusts. What does it mean for our teenagers to do the same? It means to flee the self-absorption, the despondency, the sullenness that marks this adolescent period of life. It means to run away from the sins that so easily entangle our teenagers: gossip, jealousy, anger, rebelliousness. It means to be an adolescent who desires to make a difference and is willing to pursue the things that will make that difference.

How do we help our teenagers "flee from"? How do we help them move out of the adolescent drama? We introduce realities. We remind them that their worlds are bigger than their hormones and their imaginary audiences.

Many teenagers today live in a bubble. They go to school and church and summer camps and even work with the same group of friends. Their worlds revolve around themselves and the people with whom they choose to spend their time. Therefore, they stay comfortable.

We recently spoke with a friend of ours who is a fire-fighter in New York City. He has two daughters, one who is 10 years old and one who is 15 years old. Since the attack on September 11, 2001, he has wanted to take his family to see Ground Zero. His younger daughter wants to go. She is ready. His teenage daughter, however, is afraid. "I'm scared, Dad. Someone might attack us while we're there. I'm just not ready to go to something like that yet."

"Then I guess you're not ready to go to the Britney Spears concert I got tickets for in Madison Square Garden, either."

"Well...I think I am. That could be where I start. It will be a good step back into the public for me."

Our friend chuckled as he told us this story. "We will go down to Ground Zero," he told us, "sometime soon after that concert. She needs to see it. She needs to understand what has happened."

We both loved this story. We loved it because it is such a picture of adolescence, and we loved it because this father is helping his daughter flee from youthful lusts. He is walking in wisdom and giving her choices. But he is not letting her stay comfortable. He is going to do his best to make sure she does flee, even though Britney Spears is the first step in the process.

2) *"Pursue after..."*

To pursue after is the much more exciting part of the journey. To flee from, eventually, becomes both tiresome and frustrating. Most of us can remember the games of chase that took place on the elementary school playground. Melissa has one she remembers vividly. Day after day, this one particular boy would chase her at recess. She ran and ran and ran from him. One day in the midst of the running, a thought occurred to her. She didn't have to be the one fleeing. She could be the one pursuing. So Melissa stopped, turned, and started running toward this little boy. She ran with an energy and purpose that was invigorating. She ran so hard and fast that she caught this little boy and sent him flying to the ground in a heap (and accidentally broke his arm).

That day, she understood him a little better. The running toward is much more exciting than the fleeing from. It brings about in us an energy, a vigor, and a sense of purpose that we will never find simply fleeing.

Paul tells Timothy to flee from. And then he gives him the much more exciting charge. Pursue after. Pursue after righteousness, faith, love, and peace. *It is the pursuit that brings about the purpose in our lives and the lives of our teenagers.*

We want our teenagers to begin to see life past the boredom, emptiness, weariness, and lifelessness. We want them to see that they can have a purpose.

How do we help them learn to pursue after? First, we seize every available opportunity. Rather than allowing them to be spectators, we require them to be participants. (Require is the operative word. If we ask them, they will often turn us down.)

We talk quite a bit at Daystar about teachable moments. These are the moments that occur "as we're going along." Kathleen Norris has written a book about these moments called *The Quotidian Mysteries*, describing the holiness that can be found in the ordinary. She said:

> We want life to have meaning, we want fulfill-
> ment, healing and even ecstasy, but the human
> paradox is that we find these things by starting
> where we are, not where we wish we were. We
> must look for blessings [and teachable moments]
> to come from unlikely, every day places...and
> not just spectacular events.[3]

With teenagers, we often tend to think that it takes a ropes course or a mission trip to help them have a sense of purpose. These things definitely help and have made a tremendous difference in the lives of many adolescents. But we can have mission trips and ropes courses on a daily basis when we are looking for teachable moments. They and we can find meaning in the ordinary events that occur in our lives every day.

Say you and your teenage son are driving down the road after a basketball game. The tire goes flat. Don't just tell him what to do or do it all in front of him. Draw him in. Ask him what he thinks should be done next. Make him feel that he is an important part of the process.

As we mentioned before, we always have at least one boat that breaks down at each of our summer camps. This always happens in the middle of the day when the boat is loaded with kids. Without fail, these times end up being some of the most teachable moments we have at camp. The kids step in and take ownership. They help fill the empty engine with gas. They help swim the boat to the shore. And in the midst of the helping, they always laugh and sing songs at the top of their lungs. They have a sense of purpose. In these moments, they feel a sense of meaning in their lives.

First, we look for teachable moments. And second, we praise the kids for having helped. If we were only to allow them to step in and help, they would end up resenting us. They would feel used. But when we encourage and praise them, they feel needed and useful.

Teenagers need to know their lives have purpose. We can help by giving them opportunities to live out that purpose. Send your adolescent children on mission trips. Take your family to a soup kitchen and hand out food to the homeless. Have them volunteer in the community. And don't forget to look for the opportunities in the ordinary. Seize every teachable moment as a chance to remind them that their lives have meaning. They may grunt and groan in the beginning, but they will find confidence and strength in that purpose.

A Word of Warning

In helping kids find purpose, we have found that one of the biggest stumbling blocks is often ourselves. We love our children. We want them to feel a sense of meaning and purpose. With the very best intentions, we often decide for them what their purpose should be. Even in counseling, it is easy to want to help a teenager move toward who we think they should be rather than who God is calling them to be. Parents face the same challenge. We may want our children to be artistic, musical, studious, or witty. Part of the task of loving adolescents is to help them discover and find meaning in who they are...in who God is creating them uniquely to be.

In Madeleine L'Engle's book *A Wind in the Door*, a character named Meg (who happens to be an adolescent) is introduced to a cherubim named Proginoskes. The following conversation takes place between the two of them.

"If you've been assigned to me, I suppose you must be some kind of a Namer, too, even if a primitive one."

"A what?"

"A Namer. For instance, the last time I was with a Teacher—or at school, as you call it—my assignment was to memorize the names of the stars."

"Which stars?"

"All of them."

"You mean all the stars, in all the galaxies?"

"Yes. If he calls for one of them, someone has to know which one he means. Anyhow, they like it; there aren't many who know them all by name, and if your name isn't known, then it's a very lonely feeling."

"Well, then, if I'm a Namer, what does that mean? What does a Namer do?"

The wings drew together, the eyes closed, singly, and in groups, until all were shut. Small puffs of mist-like smoke rose, swirled about him. "When I was memorizing the names of the stars, part of the purpose was to help each to be more particularly the particular star each one was supposed to be. That's basically a Namer's job. Maybe you're supposed to make earthlings feel more human."[4]

In essence, Proginoskes was naming Meg in this conversation. He was helping her be more particularly the teenager she is supposed to be.

As we know, God has created each of us with a certain uniqueness. As adults, we can help call out that uniqueness in our children. We do so by becoming Namers in their lives…by helping them find the purpose that God has specifically given them rather than the purpose we think they should have.

A Purpose Found

Four summers ago, Melissa was speaking to a group of sixth-, seventh-, and eighth-graders about worship. She was talking about how worship takes place all of the time, not just in the times that we are singing, praying, and studying the Bible. She said it is important for us to invite Jesus to be a part of all our activities...and it is when we invite Him that He comes to us.

As she was speaking, we heard a knock. One of the boys stood up and said, "Melissa, uh, I think someone's at the door."

"Okay, do you want to see who it is?"

"Sure."

He walked to the door and opened it. "Hey Jesus, come on in. We'd love to have you hang out with us today," he said.

The boy then turned to the group, smiled, and added: "Hey everybody, this is Jesus. He's my friend and He can be yours, too."

No one asked this young man to stand up and go to the door. Sitting and listening to Melissa, he had the idea. He discreetly knocked on the wall and stood up. Four years later, at every camp this young man attends, he still knocks. He stands up, goes to the door, and invites Jesus to come in and hang out with us.

In doing this small thing, this young man discovered a glimpse of what purpose feels like. He is a teenager who has been made fun of and rejected by his peers. But as soon as he walks through the doors at Daystar, his head is lifted. He feels like a leader. He knows he has something to offer and that we expect him to offer it. And he feels a confidence in the sense of purpose he has found.

As Reuben Welch wrote:

> I discovered that as I began to love people and
> care for people and become involved with
> people, I had more joy, more life, more tears,
> more laughter, more meaning, and far greater
> fun than I ever had before.[5]

This is what purpose does in the lives of our teenagers. They experience what it means to care, to love, and to offer something of themselves. They find a sense of meaning and purpose that "inspires them to new heights they know they would not reach on their own," as Os Guinness said. When we, as adults, let go of our own agendas and call out the uniqueness found in our children, we join our teenagers in their pursuit of purpose. And we have the inexpressible joy of watching as they find their own sense of purpose and meaning.

11

But...

~~~~~~~

Don't let anyone look down on you because you are young, but set an example for the believers in speech, in life, in love, in faith and in purity. Until I come, devote yourself to the public reading of Scripture, to preaching and to teaching. Do not neglect your gift...
—1 TIMOTHY 4:12-14

Teenagers use the word "but" about as often as they roll their eyes. We hear it when we ask them to do their chores— "But, Mom, I'm watching television." We hear it when they have gotten themselves into trouble—"But I'm really a good kid. I've just messed up this once. If you knew what everyone else was doing, you'd be proud of me." They use it when their grades slip—"But this teacher just gives us way too much work. No one in the class is making an A."

Adolescents can easily live in the land of excuses. Some excuses have to do with laziness, but not nearly as much as we might think. Often, something else is going on. As we have said before, adolescents are encountering an onslaught of fears and insecurities. How do they typically respond?

- "But..."

- "But I'm only 13. Why would you expect me to do something like that?"

- "But I'm afraid she'll think I'm weird."
- "But I'm too sad myself to be of help to someone else."

If we are in a relationship with an adolescent, we have most likely heard one of these excuses. They are a natural part of the teenage dialect. In this chapter, we will look at each of the "buts" that are most common: youthfulness, fear, and sadness.

We will also look at the importance of our responses to their "buts." It is easy for us to get caught up in the excuses. We have seen countless parents who prevent their children from facing the consequences of their actions, simply because they were sucked in by the "buts."

Teenagers' tendency to make excuses is overshadowed by their need to take risks. We know this fact well. Our sons tend to drive their cars entirely too fast. Our "nice" daughters often want to date boys who are rough around the edges. They love roller coasters and scary movies. All this arises out of their need to take risks. What we will assert in this chapter is that the risks that are much more frightening and more growth-producing are ones that involve our teenage children offering something of themselves.

But I'm Only a Youth

When the Lord called Jeremiah to be a prophet, Jeremiah was thought to be in his late teens. God came to Jeremiah to tell him He wanted to use him...that He wanted Jeremiah's life to have impact. Let's look at Jeremiah's response.

> *Now the word of the Lord came to me saying,*
> *"Before I formed you in the womb I knew you,*
> *And before you were born I consecrated you; I*
> *have appointed you a prophet to the nations."*

> *Then I said, "Alas, Lord God! Behold, I do*
> *not know how to speak, Because I am a youth."*
> —JEREMIAH 1:4-6 NASB

Sounds familiar, doesn't it? Jeremiah had the same response we hear often from our teenage children.

"But I'm only a youth."

Jeremiah did not believe he was capable of what the Lord was asking him to do. He had an image of himself that did not coincide with the image that God had of him.

Last summer, we drew roadmaps with a group of sixth-, seventh-, and eighth-graders. The roadmaps were symbolic pictures of their lives, and they drew peaks, valleys, and rest stops along the way. After they had finished their drawings, they each had the opportunity to come to the front of the room to share their map with the group.

The first up was a 14-year-old boy who said, "This is where my roadmap starts, when I was born. We moved when I was ten, and then last year my parents separated, so I had some valleys I had to go through. Now, things are a lot better. I like my school and play football, so that's a peak. Things are really good now."

The other kids were then given an opportunity to ask questions. "Why did your parents separate, and are you angry about it?" one of the girls asked.

"I don't really know," the boy said. "I try not to think about it. I'm just a kid. I figure I can deal with that stuff when I'm older. There's no reason to have to worry about it now."

There *is* a reason. This boy is angry. He gets into trouble in school and with his siblings because he has an anger that is always brewing beneath the surface. He needs to acknowledge his anger. But instead, this teenage boy takes a stand with Jeremiah and with countless other children his age to say, "But I'm only a youth."

This 14-year-old boy didn't want to have to deal with his feelings of anger over his parents' separation. He just wanted to have fun and enjoy "being a kid." *When something is required of teenagers beyond that for which they feel capable, they will often retreat to the safety of childhood.*

We all have images of ourselves that include who we believe ourselves to be and all that we believe we are capable of. These images are usually unspoken and often unknown even to us, but they are there. And they often affect the way that we respond to any given situation.

Teenagers are no exception. They have images of who they are. Jeremiah's image of himself was of a boy who does not speak well, particularly well enough to be "a prophet to the nations." The 14-year-old boy's image of himself is of a child—one who is free to have fun, play football, and is overwhelmed by feelings that are uncomfortable.

A Starting Point

The Bible often talks about youth with phrases such as, "from my youth," "from his youth," "from youth." In these phrases, Scripture goes back to youth as a type of starting point. We do the same in our own lives. We have said several times that many people make decisions as teenagers to accept Christ. We go back to our own adolescence as the time we really began to learn about life and relationships and began to develop our own identities. Technically, these things began in childhood. But it wasn't until we became adolescents that we were able to process with our minds all that we had taken in with our hearts up to that point.

We know adolescence is a very challenging time. Teenagers continually experience both real and imagined stress. Developmentally, they have tremendous difficulty seeing beyond themselves. But this is a starting point. This is a time they can begin to see past their teenage worlds.

Let's look at God's response to Jeremiah.

> But the Lord said to me, "Do not say, 'I am a youth,' because everywhere I send you, you shall go, And all that I command you, you shall speak. Do not be afraid of them, For I am with you to deliver you," declares the Lord. Then the Lord stretched out His hand and touched my mouth, and the Lord said to me, "Behold, I have put My words in your mouth. See, I have appointed you this day over the nations and over the kingdoms...."
>
> —JEREMIAH 1:7-10A NASB

God wanted Jeremiah to have a new image. He wanted him to have confidence and to know that he could have impact. God was strengthening Jeremiah. He did not let the conversation end in a "but." And neither should we with our adolescents. It is important for them to see that their lives can and do have impact. When we remind them of this, they will not only be strengthened, but they will also develop confidence.

But I'm Too Sad

Depression has become a part of the everyday vocabulary in today's society. Commercials that spout the life-changing benefits of antidepressants permeate the television screen. As we become a society that is much more open about feelings, we seem to be experiencing those feelings with increased depth and frequency.

In the years since we opened Daystar Counseling Ministries, there have always been kids who are sad. Their parents have gotten a divorce. Or a friend has betrayed them. Or a sibling has been killed in a car accident. For various reasons, kids have always come into our offices with a sadness that feels overwhelming.

With each year that passes, the number of these children seems to increase. More teenagers than ever before are coming in who have parents that are still married, intact friendships, and healthy siblings, but who nevertheless feel depressed. A great deal of the depression has to do with all that is happening inside of adolescents. And a great deal of the increasing number has to do with the fact that, thankfully, we now live in a society where feelings can be acknowledged.

Here we'd like to note an important difference between depression and sadness. Depression occurs when sadness is prolonged to the point that it becomes debilitating. Depression is real and is a tremendous battle to fight at any age. Because of our culture's openness, many kids and adults alike are getting help for depression who would have previously struggled in silence. For this, we are tremendously grateful.

But with every silver lining comes a cloud. The silver lining of openness about sadness and depression sometimes brings with it the cloud of being stuck. One of the reasons that teenagers (and adults) commit suicide is because they no longer believe they make a difference. They have become stuck in how they view themselves. They don't think they have significant impact. Sadness can blind us in this way.

Kids in counseling sometimes have difficulty coming into groups because of the structure of our groups. We expect every child who participates in our groups to give. Often, however, teenagers feel unable to give. They are blocked, or stuck. One of the biggest blocks we see is found in statements like these:

- "But I'm too sad."

- "How can I help anyone else when I don't know how to help myself?"

- "What could I possibly say to anyone else that would make any kind of difference?"

The image these teenagers have of themselves is that of a victim. They have acknowledged their sadness but have gotten stuck in that sadness. They no longer believe they make a difference.

A Starting Point

Where is the starting point for these adolescents? The answer is found in the very sadness that has gotten them stuck. In his play *The Angel That Troubled the Waters*, Thornton Wilder tells the story of a physician who goes each day to the pool at Bethesda to be healed of his melancholy. He sits beside the pool waiting for an angel to call him into the waters that will bring about his freedom. When his turn finally comes, the angel blocks his descent into the waters, and says these profound words:

> Without your wounds where would your power be? It is your melancholy that makes your low voice tremble into the hearts of men and women. The very angels themselves cannot persuade the wretched and blundering children on earth as can one human being broken on the wheels of living. In Love's service, only wounded soldiers can serve. Physician, draw back.[1]

The pain of these teenagers, whatever level of pain it may be, is the very thing that can bring about their compassion. Over and over we have seen that the kids who, in group, have the most impact on others are the ones who have walked through pain in their own lives.

This fact is true for all of us. Years ago in her first year at Daystar, Sissy was going through a tremendously difficult time. She was sitting in Melissa's office for her time of supervision. In the middle of it, she burst into tears about all that was going on. After she cried for a few minutes, she flipped into a state of panic.

"Oh no," she said. "I have a counseling session in five minutes. How am I ever going to talk to someone else about their problems when I'm so sad myself? I need to pull out of this right now."

"Don't you dare," said Melissa. "You walk into that office right where you are, and talk to her out of that place. Just see what happens."

That day was probably the single most life-changing day for Sissy as a counselor. Her appointment was deeply moving for her and the teenage girl with whom she met. Sissy didn't talk about her own pain but was able to respond to the girl at a level she never had before. And as a result, this young girl was able to get in touch with her own feelings that had never previously surfaced. Sissy's own pain was the starting point that brought her to greater depths of compassion as a counselor.

It is important that we help our teenage children acknowledge their pain. Talk with them when their feelings are hurt by a friend. Ask them how they feel about themselves and their insecurities. Open doors for them to connect to youth ministers, teachers, or even counselors with whom they can also talk about their feelings. Don't try to protect them from these feelings by pretending they are not there.

As they begin to acknowledge their feelings, however, be aware that they can get stuck. Find groups where your teenage children have opportunities to talk but also to give. Youth groups, discipleship groups, groups at school, and counseling groups have places where kids can connect. Help them find organizations where they also can volunteer. Encourage their compassion and demonstrate your own. You will both be changed, and they will find a much greater confidence in having walked through the pain and experienced compassion.

> *Praise be to the God and Father of our Lord Jesus Christ, the Father of compassion and the God of all comfort, who comforts us in all our troubles, so that we can comfort those in any trouble with the comfort we ourselves have received from God. For just as the sufferings of Christ flow over into our lives, so also through Christ our comfort overflows.*
>
> —2 CORINTHIANS 1:3-5

But I'm Too Afraid

Do you remember what dances were like in middle school? Parents would drop their children off in the school parking lot. Kids would walk into a gym (oops! we mean ballroom) filled with streamers and balloons. The girls would immediately rush to one side of the gym to stand in clumps. They would giggle, modestly dance around, and walk in multiples of two to the bathroom. The boys would walk in and line up on the other side of the gym. They would snicker, throw ice, and push each other. Both sides were afraid of looking foolish, and both sides were afraid of making contact. The boys were afraid to walk across the floor and ask a girl to dance. The girls were afraid they would not be asked to dance.

Last summer, Melissa talked about this with a group of high school students. She talked at length about fear and how it serves to paralyze us. Neither of us remembered that Melissa had used this illustration. We didn't remember it, that is, until the other day.

One of the students who had been a part of this group was recently brought in by his single mom. He is a young man with tremendous potential. Warm, kind, aware, and engaging—he has truly experienced God's hand in his life.

Like many boys his age, he also has become addicted to video games. He talks about them constantly with his friends at school and plays them at every opportunity. His mom grew concerned because of their content and the fact that they were taking over his free time. She started limiting when and what he could play. He then began to lie. He would sneak friends' games home and play when no one was watching. As is always the case, one lie begets another lie, and the problems increased. The lying was snowballing quickly, and his mom's concern was snowballing with it.

When they came in to meet with Sissy, his mom was at the point of despair, and he was flippant.

"What do you think is going on here?" Sissy asked him.

"I don't really know. I guess I'm in trouble for lying."

"Yes, you are. But what I want to know is why are the video games so important that you have to lie to play them?"

"I don't know."

"I'm not sure I do either. But, I'll tell you one thing. This summer, when you were at camp, you were a different guy. You held your head up, smiled, reached out to people, and had a confidence that seems to have disappeared. I think your confidence this summer came from the fact that you took some risks. You asked out a girl that you were interested in. You were vulnerable about your life with people you didn't really know. You took on a real leadership role in our group. The risks you took made you more confident. What kind of risks are you taking now?"

"I don't know. I can't think of any."

"I'm not surprised. And that's why I think you lose yourself in these video games. Instead of risking pursuing a girl or being vulnerable with a group, you are fighting pretend monsters and rescuing pretend damsels in distress. You were created to take risks, but you're no longer taking them in real life. Those video games are so important to you because they give you a counterfeit confidence."

"Yeah," he said slowly. "I guess that's exactly right. How did you figure that out? I've never thought of it that way. I can't believe you know that."

It didn't take a rocket scientist to know that this young man feels afraid. Every adolescent does, at some point or another. The fear may be of pursuing members of the opposite sex, speaking in front of a group, making a new friend, or trying out for a sport. Whatever the fear, it can be debilitating. And all of us, including teenagers, can fall into looking for ways to find counterfeit confidence when we are afraid.

For teenagers, this fear can become another "but." This young man felt some rejection from a girl and didn't want to risk pursuing another relationship. He had struggled with friends, so he found that it was safe to connect over video games.

Adolescents need adventure. Their adventures can come from video games, driving too fast, or even experimenting with drugs and alcohol. As adults who love adolescents, we want them to take different risks. We want their adventures to take place in (mostly) safe, healthy places. We want them to have courage in real life...to take risks by sitting with someone they don't know at lunch, asking out a girl, trying out for a play, or cooking a meal for their family. These types of adventures are strengthening for teenagers. They help them move past the excuse, "But I'm too afraid," and face their fears. They help them develop a true sense of confidence.

A Starting Point

The conversation with this young man moved from the risks of two-headed monsters to the risks of relationships and what it means to live with courage. Sissy told this young man: "I want you to start taking real risks again. Start small. It doesn't matter. But, I have seen who you are when you have courage and take risks. And I know you felt the difference, too. You are capable of so much more than you have any idea."

"You want me to stop throwing ice and walk across the gym floor."

"Exactly," Sissy said with a laugh.

When Melissa talked about middle school dances, she had given a challenge. This young man remembered. He had been struck, months ago, by this challenge. He was struck by it because it touched a place in him that knew he was one of the boys throwing ice. And it touched the part of him that knew he wanted to walk across that gym floor. Months later, he brought it back up.

Teenagers will have fears. It is natural. They are continually being awakened to new realities and experiences. Those can be frightening. And they are often getting their first tastes of rejection. Those can be debilitating. But we, as adults, can help get them going across the gym floor. We can prod them toward adventures of all sizes. We can remind them that they are capable...that they do have impact. And we can remind them that the greatest risks are those that take place in the midst of fear.

Life Beyond the Buts

Several years ago, Melissa was skiing with a friend and mentor, Dan Allender. They were enjoying the skiing, the beauty of the mountain, and the companionship. When they reached the bottom of the mountain, the two got in line for a very long ski lift back to the top. Once on the lift, Dan began to ask Melissa questions about her life. With each question, he took Melissa deeper and deeper into her feelings and fears. As the turnaround came at the end of the lift, Melissa was in tears. She skied off the lift, looked back at Dan and didn't say a word, but the question running through her mind was, "Now what? Here I am on top of a mountain in the middle of all this pain. So, now what?"

Just as she glanced back at Dan with her questioning look, he rushed by her in a flurry of skis and poles and shouted, "Let's ski!"

Melissa was jolted. Her vision of sitting by a fire in the restaurant nearby and talking through her pain was gone. But she sure didn't want to be left behind on top of the mountain. So she threw her "buts" to the wind and followed Dan. She still says that particular ski run was the most exhilarating experience she ever had on a ski trip.

It was exhilarating because she lived the adventure. She let go of her fears and her sadness and took a risk. She did the same thing we want our teenagers to do. We want them to taste the adventure. We want them to have the confidence that comes from learning what it means to risk—even with sadness, pain, and disappointment.

God's conversation with the teenage Jeremiah ends as God prepares Jeremiah for his own adventure. He reminds him that even in the midst of his fears, youthfulness, and pain, he still is capable. His life can and will have impact. And through every bit of the terrifying, painful, wondrous adventure, God will be with him.

> *"Get yourself ready! Stand up and say to them whatever I command you. Do not be terrified by them, or I will terrify you before them. Today I have made you a fortified city, an iron pillar and a bronze wall to stand against the whole land—against the kings of Judah, its officials, its priests and the people of the land. They will fight against you but will not overcome you, for I am with you and will rescue you," declares the Lord.*
>
> —JEREMIAH 1:17-19

Part Five

Going Out
the Back Door

12

See You Later

—

For now we must love at a distance; but God never
departs the intimate heart of a child. Never.[1]

—WALTER WANGERIN

"Goodbye, thank you. I had a nice time," we say as we
walk out the front door of someone's home. We leave the
front door after a formal visit, politely and graciously
taking our leave.

"See you later," we say as we walk out someone's back
door. "See you later," we say, knowing that we will, in fact,
see them again later. *We have a relationship that allows us to
come and go through their back door.* And that's exactly what
we do. We come and go. We leave and return. It is the
quality of our relationship with that person that gives us
the freedom to do so.

The same holds true with our teenagers. As those who
love adolescents, we have learned what it means to walk
into the back door of their hearts. We have loved them with
connection and unpredictability. We have watched and
worked alongside as God has softened, shaped, and

strengthened our children into who He is creating them to be. We have established and maintained a quality of relationship with our teenagers. We have loved them from close-up.

This chapter, however, is about loving our adolescents from a distance. It is about learning what it means to say "see you later" to our teenage children, knowing that their lives are enriched not only by our presence, but also by our absence.

Henri Nouwen wrote:

> The more experience in living we have, the more we sense that closeness grows in the continuous interplay between presence and absence. In absence, from a distance, in memory, we see each other in a new way.[2]

We will continually walk in and out the back doors of our teenagers' hearts. It is the quality and stability of our relationship that gives us the freedom to do so. And it is their need that compels us to do so.

We help our teenagers to develop as we come to understand the interplay between presence and absence. Our presence establishes the quality of relationship that gives us the freedom to be absent. And our absence gives them a chance to develop both independence and dependence that is vital to their journey toward adulthood.

Independence

"See you later" is something we will say to our children a million times as they make their way through adolescence. "See you later," we say with tremblings of fear as they get their driver's license and drive off for the first time... without us. "See you later," we whisper with sadness when they are caught cheating and have to face the consequences. "SEE YOU LATER!" we shout with pride as we watch them graduate from high school, knowing that they are embarking on a new adventure.

"See you later." Parenting teenagers is a lesson for us in what it means to hold tight and let go. We hold tight. We let go. Over and over and over. We love them from close-up and then from a distance. We are continually stepping in and out of the back door to their hearts. The stepping in lays the foundation so that we can step out. And the stepping out leads them to a sense of independence.

We recently spoke with the father of a teenage boy. He told us, "My son is just not around that much anymore. He's always off with his friends. It feels like, whenever he is home, I'm always after him. It's not that I'm trying to be critical. It's just that there's so much he needs to learn and so little time. So, I end up spending all of our time together trying to teach him those things."

This teenage son does interpret his father's teaching as criticism, simply because that is all that occurs during their interactions. There is no interplay between presence and absence. For this father to say "see you later" would not mean that he stop spending time with his son. But it would mean that he let go of trying to make sure his son is equipped with every life lesson possible. It would mean that he step out and give the lessons time and room to sink in.

Loving from a distance does not necessarily mean a physical distance. The distance is the space we give our teens to grow. Distance allows them to experience life as Henri Nouwen has talked about. It is stepping back so that they can make their own mistakes, conquer their own fears, and achieve their own accomplishments. We step out and we step in. We allow them to experience independence, but we continue to lovingly set reasonable parameters on that independence.

Dependence

We know a teenage girl with a remarkably strong sense of faith. She has truly experienced the Spirit of God on multiple occasions. She is also a young woman who has no relationship with her father. She lives with her mother, who works two jobs to support their family. In many ways, she is raising herself. If you were to ask this young woman if there is one predominant emotion she has felt throughout her growing up, she would say loneliness.

And that loneliness, she would say, has been the very thing that has propelled her toward Christ.

As those who love adolescents, we often try to prevent them from feeling lonely. We want them to be happy, to feel fulfilled, to have good friends, and to live without disappointment. These are normal desires for our children, but they are not within our control. Our children will live with disappointment, unhappiness, and loneliness at some point in their lives. And it is precisely those feelings that God can use to draw them (and us) to Himself.

Henri Nouwen said:

> I am deeply convinced that there is a ministry in which our leaving creates space for God's spirit and in which, by our absence, God can become present in a new way [p. 44]. Without this withdrawal we are in danger of no longer being the way, but in the way; of no longer speaking and acting in his name, but in ours; of no longer pointing to the Lord who sustains, but only to our own distracting personalities.[2]

Teenagers will feel loneliness and disappointment. As adults who love them, we can stand by and support them in that loneliness, but it is important that we not try to take the loneliness away. If we do, we are in danger of standing in the way of the very thing God may be using to call them to deeper dependence on Him.

Adolescence carries with it both a hunger and an ability to understand truth that wasn't there during childhood. Our children are just beginning to be able to experience for themselves the truth found in Proverbs 3:3-4:

> Let love and faithfulness never leave you; bind them around your neck, write them on the tablet of your heart. Then you will win favor and a good name in the sight of God and man.

Our absence gives our children room and time to write these truths on the tablets of their hearts. We step out so that Someone much bigger can step in.

Independence and dependence. Presence and absence. Holding on and letting go. Stepping in and out of the back door of the hearts of our teenagers as we learn to love them from a distance.

"See you later," we say, with lumps in our throats, as we give them space to grow toward adulthood. "See you later," we say, with tears in our eyes, as we watch them go through loneliness that is painful but which will ultimately bring them to a deeper sense of faith. "See you later," we ultimately say with confidence...knowing that, as Wangerin has said, we have a God who never departs the heart of a child, and knowing that we have a quality of relationship that allows us to return.

13

A Parting Thought

Melissa's brother Kim is a gifted and witty author who used to write for his hometown newspaper, *The Daily Times*. Last summer he wrote an article entitled "Garden is Now the Enemy," in which he discussed the perils of vegetable gardening. Little did he know he also could have been writing about the perils of parenting teenagers.

> In the spring we planted neat little rows of seeds and plants. We nursed them along with sweet talk and fertilizer and gentle showers of well water. I lined the little garden—about 15 by 15 feet—with a neat border of bricks, and we stood back and admired our work. We thought we had created an orderly little vegetable universe. By July the garden mocked our efforts at order. No longer could you see the brick border. Rows

were irrelevant. Cucumber vines had crawled into the yard, kudzu-like. Squash and zucchini had grown five feet tall, their leaves exploding to the size of boat cushions. To find the fruit I almost needed a machete...I'm afraid one morning I'll wake up and the melon vines will have covered my car, binding it to the driveway. Next might be the house, the thick vines locking us inside so that the vegetables can grow unchecked, unpicked, holding us hostage until the first killing frost.[1]

As adults who love adolescents, we know exactly how Kim felt about his garden. The neat little rows of children we planted have grown into wild, woolly adolescents. We feel overwhelmed and underqualified at this task of parenting, silenced by the enormity of our job. Kim goes on to say something incredibly profound, not only for gardeners, but also for those of us who care for teenagers: "I am no expert gardener."[2]

And we are no expert parents. We fail. We set out to understand our adolescents and deal with our own sin as their parents. And then we fail. We make every attempt to model simplicity and fill our homes with love and laughter. And then we fail. We try to remind them of their potential and hold their hands as we simultaneously point our fingers. And then we fail. We tell them to be thankful, have purpose, and take risks. You guessed it...we fail again.

We simply cannot be perfect parents. Neither can we grow perfect teenagers.

But we do know a few things we can do along the way. In his book *Little Lamb, Who Made Thee?*, Walter Wangerin says it best when he reminds us of the importance of coming together with laughter, conversation, and prayer as we walk this road of parenting.

> Parents, let us laugh together by telling tales of
> the idiocy of these tall children. Laughter dimin-
> ishes problems by granting a blessed release and
> a realistic perspective. Let's talk seriously, too;
> exchange advice; discover how very common,
> after all, is all that we thought bedeviled our
> family alone. And let's pray out loud. For each
> child by name. And for the parents. Because God
> is God of teenagers too. God is the one parent
> who shall not be superceded.[3]

As we gather with other parents, we are reminded that
we are not alone in this journey. We can laugh, we can talk,
and we can pray together. We can walk in and out of the
back door of our adolescents' hearts. We can rejoice as our
teenage children, each day, are molded by the Potter who is
also Parent, into who He is calling them to be.

And finally, we can breathe a sigh of relief in knowing
that there is a Master Gardener. Even when we feel like our
gardens are growing out of control, God's isn't. He has a
plan in the midst of the kudzu-like chaos. He knows and
loves each of our children much better than we do. God can
lead us to and through the back door of our teenager's
hearts. He, after all, is the One who designed them. And
He never fails.

Thanks be to God.

Notes

―――

Introduction

1. Saint Augustine, *Confessions* (Oxford, England: Oxford University Press, 1991), p. 24.

Chapter 1: Maybe You Will Know

1. Madeleine L'Engle, *A Circle of Quiet* (New York: HarperCollins, 1972), p. 33.
2. Henri Nouwen, *The Living Reminder* (New York: HarperCollins, 1977), p. 47.

Chapter 2: House of Mirrors

1. Walter Wangerin, *Reliving the Passion* (New York: HarperCollins, 1992), pp. 7–8.
2. Cindy Morgan, *Barefoot on Barbed Wire* (Eugene, OR: Harvest House Publishers, 2001), pp. 15, 19.
3. Bob Benson, *See You at The House* (Nashville, TN: Generoux Nelson, 1989), p. 126.
4. Walter Wangerin, *Reliving the Passion* (New York: Harper Collins, 1992), p. 8.

Chapter 3: Sound Tracks

1. Frederick Buechner, *Listening to Your Life* (New York: HarperCollins, 1992), pp. 4–5.
2. Rosie O'Donnell, "A Teacher for Life," *Rosie*, September 2001, pp. 56–57.
3. Dan Allender, *The Healing Path* (Colorado Springs, CO: WalterBrook Press, 1999), p. 31.
4. Anne Lamott, *Bird by Bird* (New York: Pantheon Books, 1994), p. 116.
5. Eugene Peterson, *Living the Message* (New York: HarperCollins, 1996), p. 111.
6. Mike Mason, *The Mystery of Children* (Colorado Springs, CO: WaterBrook Press, 2001), p. 243.
7. Willa Cather, *Death Comes for the Archbishop* (New York: Random House, 1927, 1955), p. 50.

8. Larry Crabb, *Connecting* (Nashville, TN: Word Publishing, 1997), pp. 4–5.
9. Ibid.

Chapter 4: In Here and Out There

1. Nancy Gibbs, "Who's in Charge Here?," *Time*, August 6, 2001, pp. 41.
2. Ibid., p. 46.
3. Brennan Manning, *Abba's Child* (Colorado Springs, CO: NavPress, 1994), p. 23.
4. William R. Newell, *Hebrews Verse by Verse* (Chicago: Moody Press, 1947), p. 207.
5. Madeleine L'Engle, *Walking on Water* (Wheaton, IL: Harold Shaw Publishers, 1980), p. 76.

Chapter 5: Stargazing

1. Adapted from "*A Song of Simplicity*" as published in *Polishing the Petoskey Stone.* Copyright © 1990 by Luci Shaw. Used by permission of WaterBrook Press, Colorado Springs, CO. All rights reserved.
2. Kim Thomas, *Simplicity* (Nashville, TN: Broadman & Holman Publishers, 1999), p. 2.
3. David Noonan, "Stop Stressing Me," *Newsweek*, January 29, 2001, pp. 54–55.
4. Gail Godwin, *Evensong* (New York: Ballantine Books, 1999), p. 48.
5. Madeleine L'Engle and Luci Shaw, *Friends for the Journey* (Ann Arbor, MI: Vine Books, 1997), p. 125.

Chapter 6: Love and Laughter

1. G.K. Chesterton, *All Things Considered* (Philadelphia: Dufour, 1969), pp.141–142.
2. Bob Benson, *See You at the House* (Nashville, TN: Generoux Nelson, 1989), pp. 254–255.
3. Eugene Peterson, *A Long Obedience in the Same Direction* (Downers Grove, IL: InterVarsity Press, 2000), p. 97.
4. Dan Allender and Tremper Longman III, *Cry of the Soul* (Colorado Springs, CO: NavPress, 1994), p. 152.
5. Jan Struther, *Mrs. Miniver* (San Diego, CA: Harcourt Brace Jovanovich, Publishers, 1939), p. 116.

Chapter 7: A Great Big Bundle of Potentiality

1. "I Am a Promise," Words by William J. and Gloria Gaither, music by William J. Gaither. Copyright © 1975 Gaither Music Company. All rights controlled by Gaither Copyright Management. Used by permission.
2. Lawrence O. Richards, *Expository Dictionary of Bible Words* (Grand Rapids, MI: Zondervan, 1985), p. 604.
3. Sharon Begley, "Mind Expansion: Inside the Teenage Brain," in *Newsweek*, May 8, 2000, p. 68.
4. Elizabeth Goudge, *The Scent of Water* (New York: Coward-McCann, Inc., 1963), p. 194.
5. Caroline J. Simon, *The Disciplined Heart* (Grand Rapids, MI: William B. Eerdmans Publishing Company, 1997), p. 16.

Chapter 8: Holding Their Hands, Pointing Our Fingers

1. Karen Mains, *Comforting One Another* (Nashville, TN: Thomas Nelson Publishers, 1997), p. 70.
2. Frederick Buechner, *Whistling in the Dark* (San Francisco: HarperCollins, 1988), p. 119.

3. Rebecca Manley Pippert, *Hope Has Its Reasons* (Downers Grove, IL: InterVarsity Press, 1989), p. 160.
4. George MacDonald, *The Curate's Awakening* (Minneapolis, MN: Bethany House Publishers, 1985), p. 80.

Chapter 9: A Thankful Heart

1. Thomas Merton, *Thoughts in Solitude* (New York: Farrar, Straus, and Giroux, 1958), p. 33.
2. Henri Nouwen, *The Return of the Prodigal Son* (New York: Image Books by special arrangement with Doubleday, 1994), pp. 85–86.
3. Eugene Peterson, *A Long Obedience in the Same Direction* (Downers Grove, IL: InterVarsity Press, 2000), p. 194.

Chapter 10: Bridge of Hope

1. Os Guinness, *Long Journey Home* (Colorado Springs, CO: WaterBrook Press, 2001), p. 208.
2. Ibid., p. 2.
3. Kathleen Norris, *The Quotidian Mysteries* (New York: Paulist Press, 1998), p. 12.
4. Madeleine L'Engle, *A Wind in the Door* (New York: Bantam Doubleday Dell Publishing Group, 1973), pp. 77–78.
5. Reuben Welch, *We Really Do Need Each Other* (Nashville, TN: Generoux Nelson, 1973), p. 92.

Chapter 11: But...

1. Thornton Wilder, *The Angel That Troubled the Waters and Other Plays* (New York: Coward-McCann, 1928), p. 20.

Chapter 12: See You Later

1. Walter Wangerin, *Little Lamb, Who Made Thee?* (Grand Rapids, MI: Zondervan Publishing House, 1993), pp. 146–147.
2. Henri Nouwen, *The Living Reminder* (New York: HarperCollins, 1977), pp. 39–40, 44, 47–48.

Chapter 13: A Parting Thought

1. Kim Trevathan, "Blount Rambling," *The Daily Times*, August, 2001.
2. Ibid.
3. Walter Wangerin, *Little Lamb, Who Made Thee?* (Grand Rapids, MI: Zondervan Publishing House, 1993), pp. 146–147.

Other Good
Harvest House Reading

HELP! MY LITTLE GIRL'S GROWING UP
by Annette Smith

With big doses of humor and lots of practical tips, author Annette Smith guides you through the often tumultuous teen years when your little girl becomes a woman. You'll learn how to enhance communication with your daughter, deepen her Christian faith, and boost her confidence.

HELP! MY LITTLE BOY'S GROWING UP
by Annette Smith

In this sequel to the popular *Help! My Little Girl's Growing up*, Annette Smith will skillfully guide you along the path of a boy's physical changes, his relational challenges, and his experiences at school, at play, and at work. Each chapter concludes with a fun and helpful list of practical, creative ways that you and your son can enjoy these important years together.

THE POWER OF A PRAYING® PARENT
by Stormie Omartian

In 30 short, easy-to-read chapter, award-winning singer and songwriter Stormie Omartian shares how you can pray through every age and stage of your child's life. Learn how to turn to the Father and place every detail of your child's life in His loving and capable hands.

10 THINGS I WANT MY DAUGHTER TO KNOW
by Annie Chapman

Drawing on her years of being a mother, the wisdom of God's Word, and the practical insights of other moms, Annie Chapman encourages mothers to consider 10 essential truths to share with their daughters.

10 THINGS I WANT MY SON TO KNOW
by Steve Chapman

Turning to the "manuel" that comes with children (the Bible), best-selling author Steve Chapman shares the principles and life wisdom that shaped his attitudes about being a dad and guided him to raising a respectful son dedicated to the Lord.